HAND PUPPETS

How to Make and Use Them

Written and Illustrated by

Laura Ross

DOVER PUBLICATIONS, INC., New York

For Ethna Sheehan

The puppets were made by the author, using the method described in this book.

Photographs courtesy of George Dec Studios

Published in Canada by General Publishing Company, Ltd., 30 Lesmill Road, Don Mills, Toronto, Ontario.
Published in the United Kingdom by Constable and Company, Ltd., 10 Orange Street, London WC2H 7EG.

This Dover edition, first published in 1989, is an unabridged, slightly corrected republication of the work originally published by the Lothrop, Lee & Shepard Co., New York, 1969.

Manufactured in the United States of America
Dover Publications, Inc., 31 East 2nd Street, Mineola, N.Y. 11501

Library of Congress Cataloging-in-Publication Data

Ross, Laura.
    Hand puppets : how to make and use them / written and illustrated
      by the author.
        p.   cm.
    Reprint. Originally published: Lothrop, Lee & Shepard Co., c1969.
    Includes bibliographical references.
    Summary: Directions and diagrams for making various types of
      puppets, dressing and handling them, setting up a stage, and
      writing and producing one's own show. Includes three puppet
      plays.
    ISBN 0-486-26161-1
    1. Hand puppets—Juvenile literature.   2. Puppet making—Juve-
    nile literature.   [1. Puppet plays.]   I. Title.
PN1972.R59   1989
791.5'3—dc20   89-38965
                                                                       CIP
                                                                       AC

Contents

Foreword

This book was planned for beginning puppeteers and also for those who have had some experience with puppets. Its aim is to show how to make simple paper bag puppets, rod puppets, and papier-mâché puppets; how to write a puppet play and produce a puppet show.

Here you will find the type of puppets which the children in my school library have made and used. We learned together, through experience, how to work with puppets, and what is necessary and what to avoid.

These pages will show you from beginning to end how to make three basic types of puppets, how to dress them, how to handle them, how to write your own play or adapt a folk tale for your very own show, how to set up a stage, and how to produce a play.

Puppets are most exciting little characters. You do not need to have special talent or skill to create them. If you have the most important requirement of a puppeteer, which is a great desire to put on a puppet show, the next thing that is needed is a certain amount of know-how. Once this is learned, it becomes easy and challenging to create puppets and use them.

There is no one way of making any puppet. There are simply certain basic steps to know, which can be modified by using your creative imagination.

Here are set forth step-by-step directions and diagrams. But do not hesitate to alter and improvise as you think of other possibilities. It is hoped that the following pages will help children, teachers, and parents to experience the joys of creating and staging puppet shows.

Introduction

People have been making puppets for thousands of years. In ancient times when Egypt, Greece, and Rome ruled the western world, puppets were meant for adults only. They were used in religious ceremonies and often buried in ancient tombs. At about the same time, people of Mexico and the primitive American Indians were also familiar with puppets. They, too, used puppets mainly for religious purposes.

The rich folklore of ancient India used puppets to tell stories. Among the early inhabitants of Persia, Turkey, Siam, Java, and Burma puppets and puppeteers held honored positions. In some of these lands puppeteers rank

9

high in society even to this day. In the Latin countries (France, Italy, Spain) puppeteers are still extremely popular with adults.

In ancient China and Japan the puppet was equally well known and was used to tell stories of the daily happenings of the people. The authors of the countless puppet plays were held in the highest esteem. Chinese and Japanese puppeteers were skillfully trained. In the eighteenth century the most famous playwrights in Japan wrote for the puppet theater. The art they acquired was passed on from one generation to the next, as a treasured, lifetime gift.

When Christianity was still new, puppets were first used in the churches of Italy, then later in France, to tell religious stories. However, because puppeteers turned more and more to stories of the world, rather than of religion, they were expelled from the church. But this did not discourage the puppeteers at all. They took to performing in the streets of the market places and soon became popular entertainers. In the Middle Ages, puppets were the most popular entertainment for the great masses of people.

The puppeteers went all over Europe with their puppets. They were welcomed in Puritan England, where all the theaters had been closed. Each country had names of their own for their favorite puppets. The best known of these became Guignol and Polichinelle in France; Pulcinella, Pantalone and Arlecchino in Italy; Hanswurst and Kasperle in Germany and Austria; Petrushka in Russia; Pulichinela in Spain; and Punch and Judy in England.

Punch and Judy migrated to the U.S. with the English immigrants but did not immediately enjoy popularity. The German puppets never really became popular in

America since they were more like stunt and trick characters than the traditional folk characters. The Italian puppeteer set up his stage among people of his own nationality. Here were enjoyed the legends of Orlando Furioso which had been traditional in Italy for centuries.

It was not until the coming of television that puppet shows were enjoyed by both children and adults on a large scale. Puppet performances are now given in the theaters as well as on TV and are being enjoyed by people of all ages.

More and more, this ancient art is gaining popularity among school children. Interest in puppetry provides students with an opportunity to work creatively by modeling and dressing puppets, building stages, and writing original puppet stories or retelling folk tales.

Materials and Sources

Most of the materials needed for making many types of puppets, such as construction paper, colored felt, cardboard, glue, tempera paints, shellac, brushes, dowels, and rods, can be obtained at a good hobby shop or art-supply store.

Powdered wallpaper glue can be bought at a hardware or paint store for very little. Masonite is available at lumberyards, where it can be cut to the required size.

Paper bags in all sizes come free with your food purchases at the local market. From the same source you can also get cardboard boxes for puppet stages.

Much can be found in your home. For puppet making, cultivate the habit of keeping a scrap box in which to store such items for future use as: scraps of material, old rags, discarded cotton dresses, blouses, and pajamas to make puppet dresses, buttons, ribbons, feathers, rickrack, pipe cleaners, paper doilies, and so on. With permission, you can borrow hammer and nails from your father's workbench. Adhesive tape for attaching scenery and props can be found in the medicine cabinet.

Save old telephone books to tear and use for papiermâché puppets, also the cardboard tubes from empty rolls of toilet tissue for constructing puppet necks. Cardboard from old shoe boxes is valuable, too.

Don't feel that you must buy every item you need. See how resourceful you can be by using anything that comes your way that suggests puppet making to you.

Directions for Tracing

1. Place tracing paper over the drawing in the book, extending the paper beyond the edges of the book.
2. Fasten the tracing paper with Scotch Tape or masking tape directly onto the table on which you are working.
3. Trace the drawing with your pencil. Be sure you do not press too hard on the paper or you will cut through it with your pencil point.
4. Trace all solid and dotted lines. Dotted lines indicate bending or cutting lines.

   Note. These first four steps are to be followed only when you are making paper patterns.
5. When you have completed all the necessary tracing, remove the tracing paper from the book. For transferring the drawing onto construction paper, turn it over to its reverse side. Lay it on a large piece of scrap paper.
6. With the flat side of a soft pencil, shade over all the lines.
7. Turn it right side up again, facing you.
8. Place it over the construction or cardboard paper.
9. Hold the two firmly together with a small piece of Scotch Tape or masking tape.
10. With your pencil, retrace the whole drawing on the construction or cardboard paper.
11. Remove the tracing paper and check against the drawing in the book. If any lines have been omitted, draw them in.
12. Cut along all solid lines with a scissors.
13. When dotted lines are to be folded, score them lightly first with the point of a nail file or scissors. When dotted lines are to be cut, the directions in the text will tell you so.

List of Terms

BACKDROP.   A sheet of paper hung across the back of a stage for scenery. It can also be a background cloth for actors.

BASTE.   To sew with long stitches in order to hold two pieces of cloth together temporarily.

CUE WORDS.   The last few words of an actor's speech in a play, which serve as a signal for another actor to start speaking. This promotes continuity of the play.

CYLINDER.   A tube, longer than it is wide, that can serve as a neck for a puppet.

DIALOGUE.   The conversation of two or more characters in a play.

DOWEL.   A round rod or stick, used in puppetry for fitting into a hole in the base of a stand, or for attaching to a rod puppet.

DRAMA.   A story told in play form.

HEM.   A border, folded twice and stitched down, usually at the bottom of a dress.

PLAY.   A story acted on the stage.

PLOT.   The plan of a story or play.

PROPERTIES.   Objects, other than scenery and costumes, that are used in a play.

PROSCENIUM.   The part of a stage that is in front of the curtain.

ROD.   A straight, slender stick that is attached to a cardboard puppet to hold it upright.

SCREEN.   A translucent shade necessary for a shadow-puppet play. It divides the audience from the puppets and the source of light.

SCRIPT.   A written story of a play presented in dialogue form. It must show title, list of characters, list of properties, and statement explaining the setting and what happens at curtain rise.

THEME.   The subject of a story or play.

Paper Bag
{1} Puppets

Of all the different types of puppets, the paper bag puppet is one of the simplest and most enjoyable to make. The bag can be used in two basic ways:

1. Empty—with decorations on it.
2. Stuffed—with toweling or newspaper for the head.

The Empty Paper Bag Puppet. This can be constructed in two ways:

1. The bottom flap of the bag, which is also the bottom of the bag, can be used to locate the top part of the mouth, while the bottom part of the mouth is located directly underneath it, where the bottom edge of the flap meets the front of the bag (see diagram).

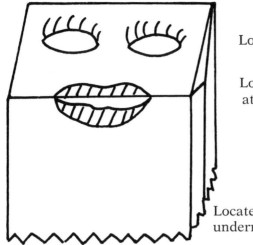

Locate eyes on flap of bag.

Locate top of mouth
at bottom of flap.

Locate bottom of mouth directly
underneath on front of bag.

By placing the four fingers of your hand inside the flap so that the tips of your fingers rest on the bottom fold, you can move the flap up and down against the palm of your hand. This will cause the upper lip of the mouth to meet with the lower lip, giving the impression that the puppet is speaking. The eyes are placed farther up on the flap of the bag and do not move.

2. Another way to use an empty paper bag is for the flap to contain the eyelids and eyelashes at the fold instead of the upper lip. The eyes themselves are constructed be-

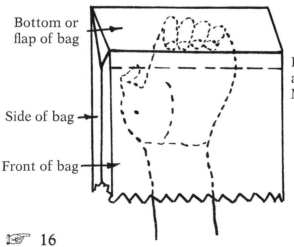

Bottom or
flap of bag

Rest tips of fingers
at edge of fold.
Move flap up and down.

Side of bag

Front of bag

neath the flap on the front of the bag. Moving the flap with your fingers and palm, will give the impression that the eyes are opening and closing. With this type of construction, the mouth is located farther down on the front of the bag and cannot be made to move.

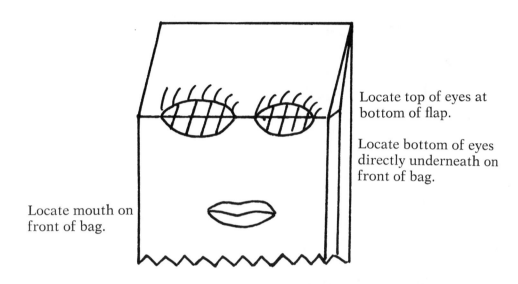

Locate top of eyes at bottom of flap.

Locate bottom of eyes directly underneath on front of bag.

Locate mouth on front of bag.

Puppet features may be drawn directly onto the paper bag. But a more interesting puppet results when features and decorations are made with bits of colored felt, construction paper, wool, absorbent cotton, buttons, rickrack, and feathers, among other materials.

The Stuffed Paper Bag Puppet. This is very simple to construct. The bottom of the bag is stuffed with crushed paper toweling or newspaper. I prefer to use paper toweling because it is softer and more easily handled than newspaper. After stuffing the bottom of the bag as large as you want the head to be, tie a string around the bag

17

under the stuffing. Pinch and shape with your fingers as much as needed. If the puppet is to be an old man, work a few creases on the face.

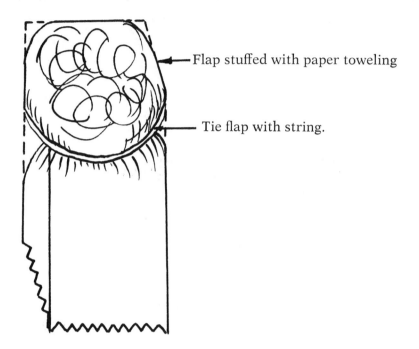

Flap stuffed with paper toweling

Tie flap with string.

You can, if you wish, draw the features with crayon, but for a more lifelike puppet, use bits of felt and other materials.

Before constructing a paper bag puppet, think about the role it will have in the play. This will help you to decide on the type to make. There are many things about a character in a ready-made story or play which will determine the kind of paper bag puppet to make.

For example, will it talk a great deal? If it will, then a paper bag with its mouth opening and closing should be made. If not, then a bag with its eyes opening and closing could be made. In the case of a king or queen, crowns should be made for them to wear to keep them in character. Since it is difficult to make a round crown for a flat bag, it would be best to make the stuffed bag puppet which is more suitable for a crown.

Also, before constructing the puppet, visualize what you want it to look like. Draw a rough sketch on paper, blocking out the details before starting.

Further on you will find directions for making the different types of paper bag puppets for the play *Rumpelstiltskin*, which you will find on page 157.

The materials listed are the ones I have used in making my puppets. However, you may prefer to use different materials and different colors.

Directions for Making Rumpelstiltskin Paper Bag Puppet for Rumpelstiltskin

Materials Needed

Paper bag 6¼ inches by 13¼ inches
Scissors
Pins
Black, yellow, red, and blue felt,
or construction paper
Two small wooden ice-cream spoons
Four small wooden cake forks
Elmer's Glue-All or Sobo glue
Tracing paper
Pencil

Directions to Follow

1. Draw a rough sketch on paper, blocking out the parts with some details before starting to work. Remember that Rumpelstiltskin does a great deal of talking. Therefore, it would be best to construct him so that his mouth opens and shuts. He is a supernatural character, so let your imagination run free.

2. Lay bag flat on table with flap open. The underneath part of the flap will become the inner portion of the upper mouth. The front of the bag directly under it will become the inner portion of the lower mouth.

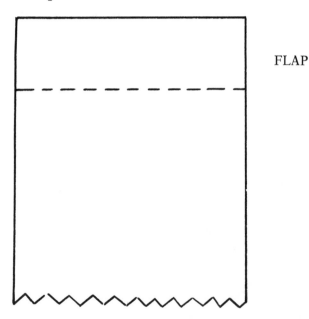

FLAP

Lay bag flat on table with flap open.

3. For the puppet's beard, trace the diagram (see Directions for Tracing, 1 to 4, in front of book). Cut pattern. Pin pattern on piece of black felt. Cut around pattern.

Cut dotted lines. Also cut notches along top edge. Remove pins.

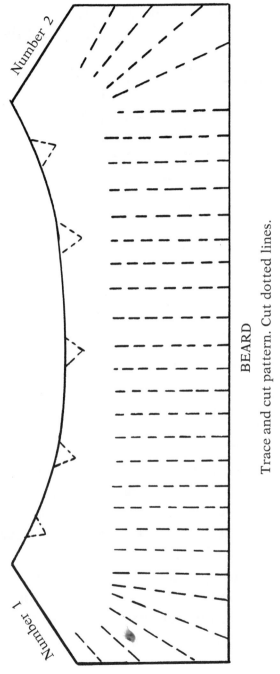

Number 2

Number 1

BEARD

Trace and cut pattern. Cut dotted lines.

4. Apply glue on beard along top edge and sides one and two. Attach beard to front of bag so that sides one and two will lie along the line where the bottom edge of flap will meet with it when closed. This will spread the cut part of beard as shown.

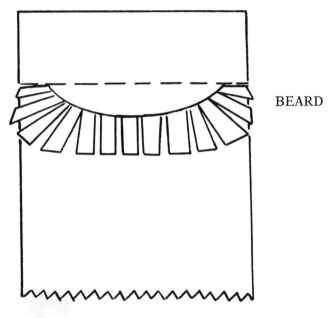

BEARD

Glue beard and attach to front
of bag as directed.

5. For the first lining of puppet's mouth, trace the diagram. Cut pattern. Pin pattern on piece of yellow felt. Cut around pattern. Remove pins.
6. Put glue on yellow lining around edges and attach underneath flap of bag so that top and side edges coincide with the edges of the opened flap and the lower curved edge is resting slightly over the black beard (see page 24).
7. For the second mouth lining, trace the diagram on page 24. Cut pattern. Pin pattern on red felt. Cut around pattern. Remove pins.

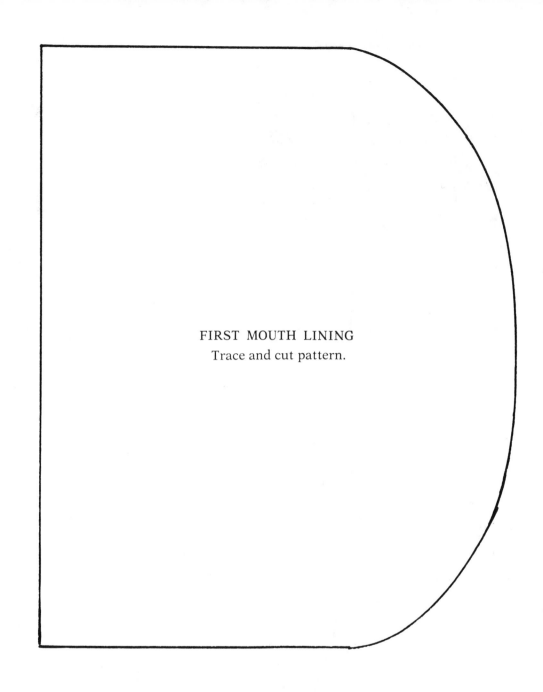

FIRST MOUTH LINING
Trace and cut pattern.

8. Put glue along edge and attach to yellow lining so that one tip of the oval rests at center of top edge of underside of flap as shown on page 25.

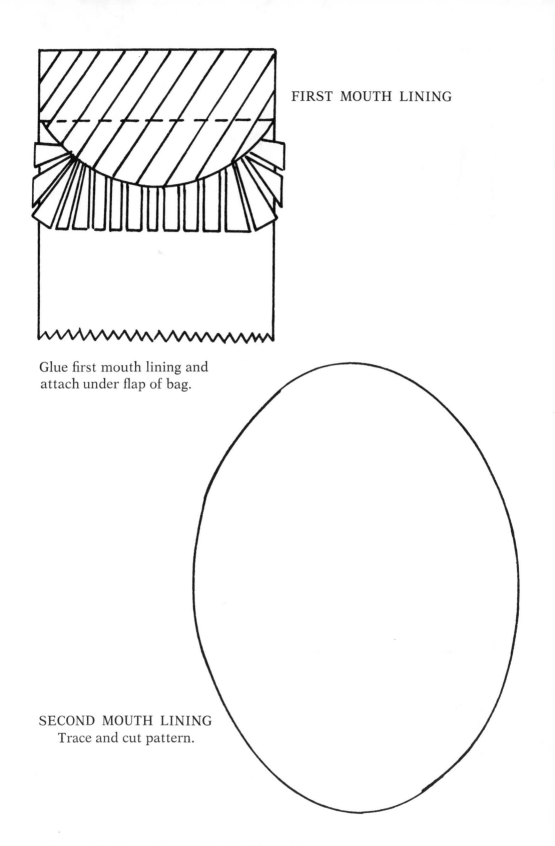

FIRST MOUTH LINING

Glue first mouth lining and
attach under flap of bag.

SECOND MOUTH LINING
Trace and cut pattern.

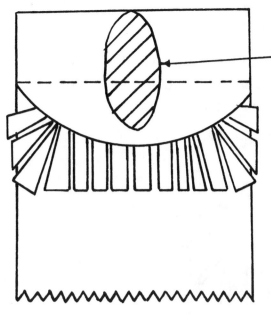

SECOND MOUTH LINING

Glue second mouth lining and attach over the first one.

9. For puppet's tongue, use a wooden spoon. Line it by gluing a piece of red felt over one side and when dry cut around.

10. Put glue on unlined side and attach to center part of second mouth lining so that the bottom tip lies slightly over black beard as shown.

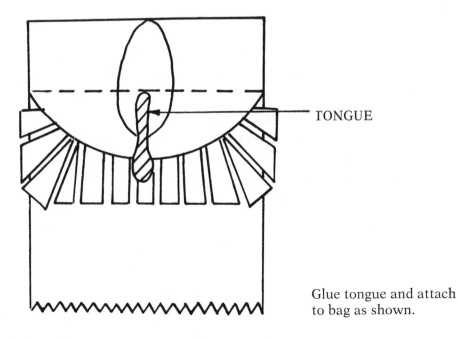

TONGUE

Glue tongue and attach to bag as shown.

11. For teeth, break off handle of two wooden forks. Put glue on one side of each and attach to second mouth lining, one on each side of the tongue as shown.

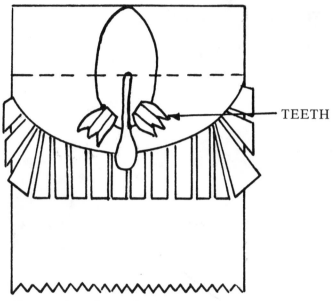

Glue teeth and attach to
second mouth lining as shown.

12. Close flap of bag.
13. For nose, use a wooden spoon. Line it by gluing a piece of yellow felt on one side and when dry, cut around.
14. Put glue on the unlined side. Attach to closed flap so that the top end is attached to the top edge of the closed flap and the curved bottom end of spoon falls partly over the tongue as shown.
15. For eyebrows, trace pattern. Cut pattern. Pin pattern to two pieces of red felt. Cut around pattern. Remove pins.
16. For eyelashes, use wooden forks (one for each eye).

Break off handles. Put glue on one side and attach over lower straight edge of eyebrows as shown.

17. For eyes, trace pattern. Cut pattern. Pin pattern to two pieces of blue felt. Cut around pattern. Remove pins.

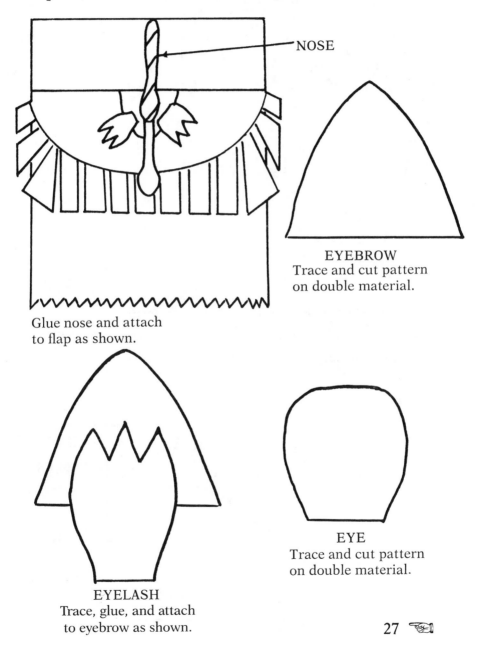

NOSE

Glue nose and attach
to flap as shown.

EYEBROW
Trace and cut pattern
on double material.

EYELASH
Trace, glue, and attach
to eyebrow as shown.

EYE
Trace and cut pattern
on double material.

18. Put glue on one side of felt, and attach to wooden eyelashes so that the ragged edges of fork protrude as shown.

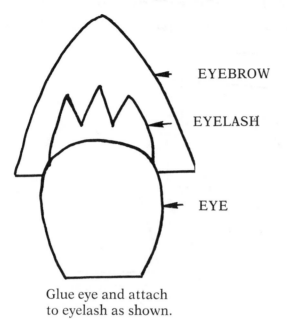

EYEBROW

EYELASH

EYE

Glue eye and attach
to eyelash as shown.

19. For pupil of eyes, cut two small round pieces of yellow felt. Put glue on one side of each and attach to lower edge of blue felt as shown.

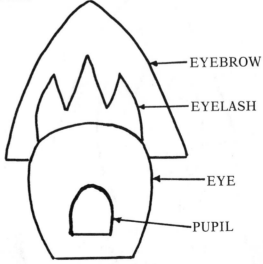

EYEBROW

EYELASH

EYE

PUPIL

Glue pupil and attach
to eye as shown.

20. Put glue on back of all attached pieces and attach to closed flap at appropriate places, one on each side of nose so that the tops of eyebrows lie at top edge of flap as shown.

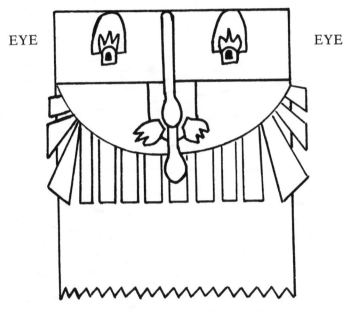

EYE   EYE

Glue eyes and attach to flap as shown.

21. For puppet's hair, trace and cut pattern on page 30. Pin it to black or red felt. Cut around pattern. Cut along dotted lines. Remove pins.

22. Put glue on top edge of felt. Attach it to back of flap at top edge so that the cut strips fall over puppet's face. Your Rumpelstiltskin puppet is now complete.

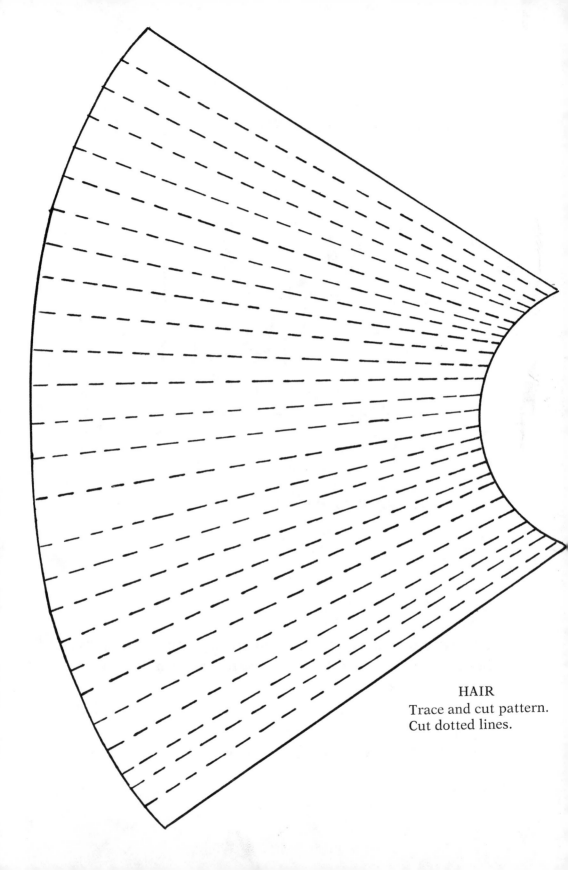

HAIR
Trace and cut pattern.
Cut dotted lines.

Glue hair and attach from back of bag.

Mouth line will open and close.

COMPLETED PAPER BAG PUPPET FOR RUMPELSTILTSKIN

Directions for Making the Miller Paper Bag Puppet for Rumpelstiltskin

Materials Needed

Paper bag 6¼ inches by 13¼ inches
Yellow, blue, black, and red felt
or construction paper
Black yarn
Black or blue construction paper
Pencil
Scissors
Tracing paper
Pins
Elmer's Glue-All or Sobo glue

Directions to Follow

1. Draw a small rough sketch with some attention to details. Since the miller appears for a short while and doesn't have very much to say, we will make the paper bag puppet with eyes that open and shut.

2. Lay the bag flat on table with flap in closed position.

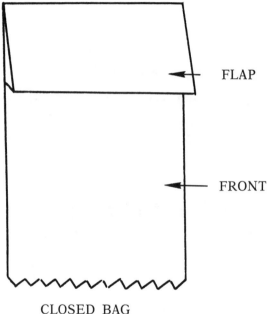

FLAP

FRONT

CLOSED BAG

3. For eyelids, trace diagram (see Directions for Tracing, 1 to 4, in front of book). Cut pattern. Pin pattern on two pieces of blue felt. Cut around pattern. Remove pins.

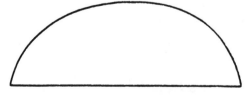

EYELID
Trace and cut pattern on double material.

4. Put glue on one side of each and attach straight edge on bottom edge of flap as shown.

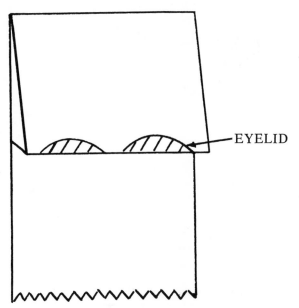

Glue eyelid and attach to edge of flap as shown.

5. For eyebrows, trace diagram. Cut pattern. Pin pattern on two pieces of yellow felt. Cut around pattern. Remove pins.

EYEBROW

Trace and cut pattern on double material.

6. Put glue on one side of each and attach over eyelids as shown on page 34.

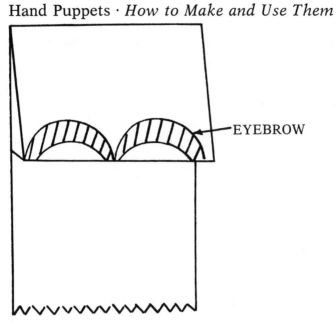

EYEBROW

Glue eyebrow and attach above eyelid as shown.

7. For eye backing, crumble two small pieces of paper toweling in oval shape and glue each on front of bag just underneath the bottom edge of flap. Part of the paper should be concealed by the bottom edge of the flap.

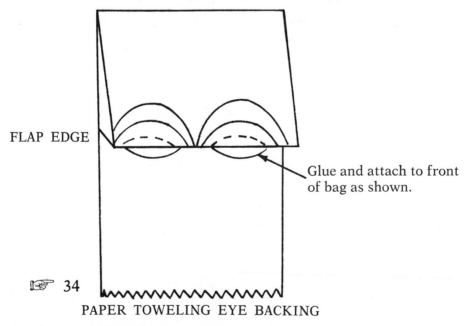

FLAP EDGE

Glue and attach to front of bag as shown.

34

PAPER TOWELING EYE BACKING

8. For eyes, trace diagram. Cut pattern. Pin pattern to two pieces of yellow felt. Cut around pattern. Remove pins.
9. For pupils, cut two small pieces of red felt in diamond shape and glue each over center of yellow eyes.

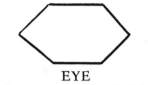

EYE
Trace and cut pattern on double material.

10. Put glue on reverse side of each eye and superimpose over the crumpled pieces of paper toweling as shown. This will bring the eyes out from the surface of the bag and give them an appearance of depth.

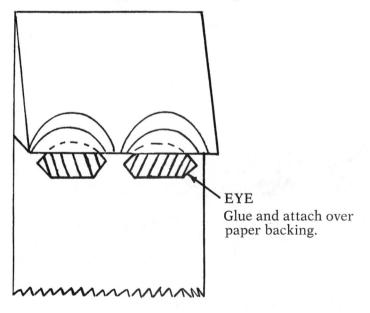

EYE
Glue and attach over
paper backing.

11. For eyelashes, trace the diagram. Cut pattern. Pin pattern on two pieces of black felt. Cut around pattern. Remove pins.

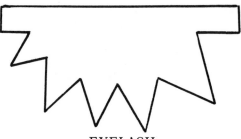

EYELASH
Trace and cut pattern on double material.

12. Put glue on upper edge of each on one side. Attach each to the underneath bottom edge of flap so that when closed the eyelashes will lie over the eyes as shown.

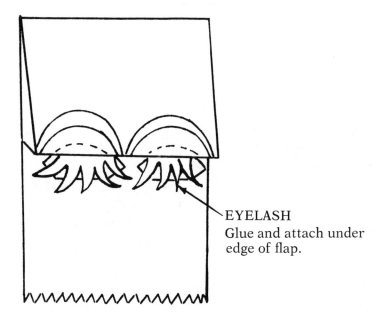

EYELASH
Glue and attach under edge of flap.

13. For puppet's nose, trace the diagram and transfer it to blue construction paper (see Directions for Tracing, 1 to 13, in front of book).

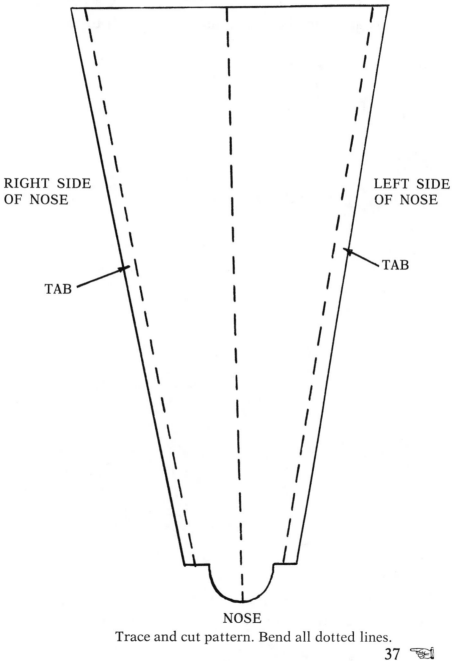

RIGHT SIDE
OF NOSE

LEFT SIDE
OF NOSE

TAB

TAB

NOSE
Trace and cut pattern. Bend all dotted lines.

37

14. Put glue along tabs on right and left side of nose. Attach to face so that wide bridge of nose lies between the eyes as shown. Be sure that the fold down the center comes away from the bag, thus giving depth to the nose.

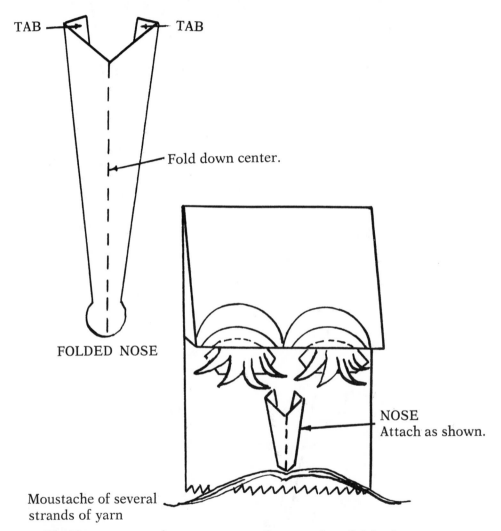

TAB

TAB

Fold down center.

FOLDED NOSE

NOSE
Attach as shown.

Moustache of several strands of yarn

15. For moustache, cut several strands of black yarn 9 inches long. Arrange into a bundle. Put glue at center of bundle, then attach under nose.

16. For mouth, trace diagram. Cut pattern. Pin pattern on red felt. Cut around pattern. Remove pins.

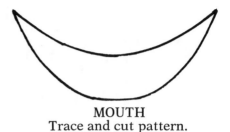

MOUTH
Trace and cut pattern.

17. Put glue on one side and attach under moustache as shown.

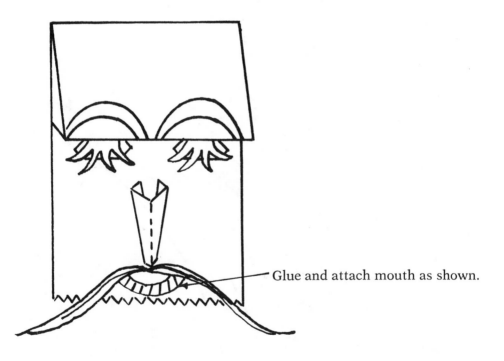

Glue and attach mouth as shown.

18. For hair, trace diagram and transfer to black construction paper. Cut along dotted lines (see page 40).

39

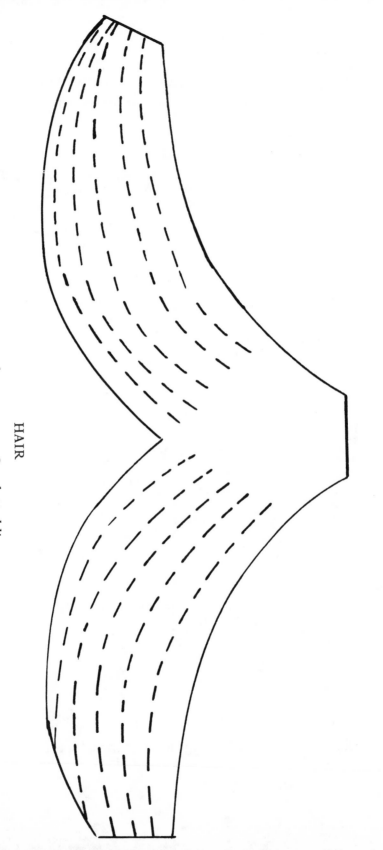

HAIR
Trace and cut pattern. Cut dotted lines.

19. Apply glue to top and center of one side and attach to back and top of flap so that hair folds over the top edge of flap as shown. Your puppet is now complete.

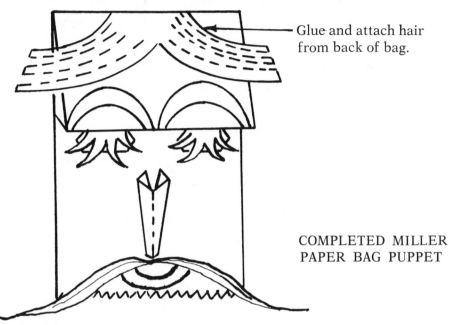

Glue and attach hair from back of bag.

COMPLETED MILLER
PAPER BAG PUPPET

Directions for Making the Messenger Paper Bag Puppet for Rumpelstiltskin

Materials Needed

Paper bag 6 ¼ inches by 13 ¼ inches
Scissors
Pins
Red, blue, black, and green felt
or construction paper
Yellow, black, and white construction paper
Elmer's Glue-All or Sobo glue
Tracing paper
Pencil

Directions to Follow

1. Draw a rough sketch of puppet's head on paper, blocking out the general shape before starting to work. He will be an empty bag puppet with a mouth that opens and shuts.

2. Lay bag flat on table with flap in open position. The underneath part of the flap will become the messenger's inner upper mouth. The front of the bag directly under it will become the inner lower mouth, as shown.

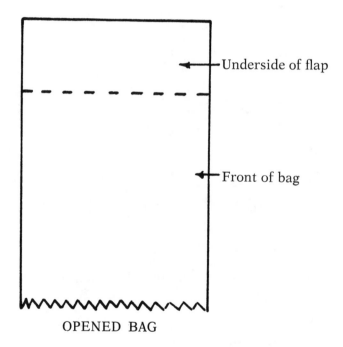

— Underside of flap

— Front of bag

OPENED BAG

3. For lining of messenger's mouth, trace the diagram (see Directions for Tracing, 1 to 4, in front of book). Cut pattern. Pin pattern on piece of red felt. Cut around pattern. Remove pins.

LINING OF MESSENGER'S MOUTH
Trace and cut pattern.

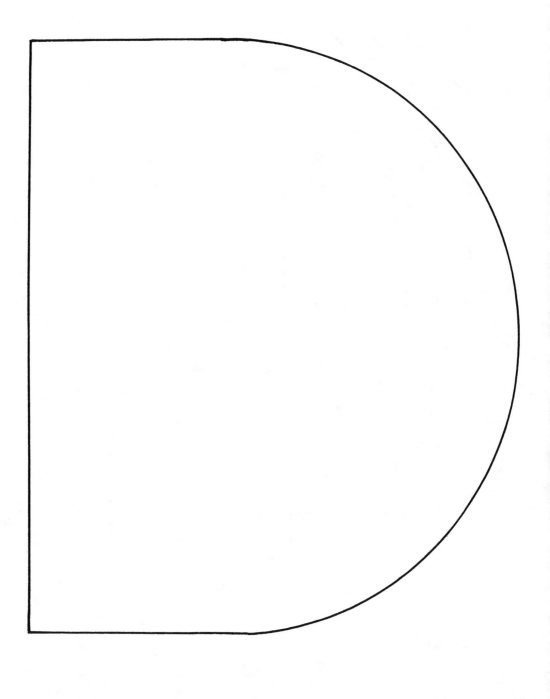

4. Put glue on one side and attach to bag as shown.

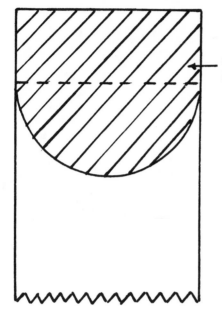

— Glue lining of mouth and attach as shown.

5. For puppet's upper teeth, trace diagram and transfer to yellow construction paper (see Directions for Tracing, 1 to 12 in front of book).

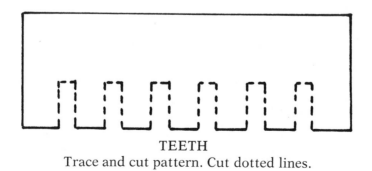

TEETH
Trace and cut pattern. Cut dotted lines.

6. Put glue on one side along straight edge and attach to center part of inner upper edge of mouth lining, as shown.

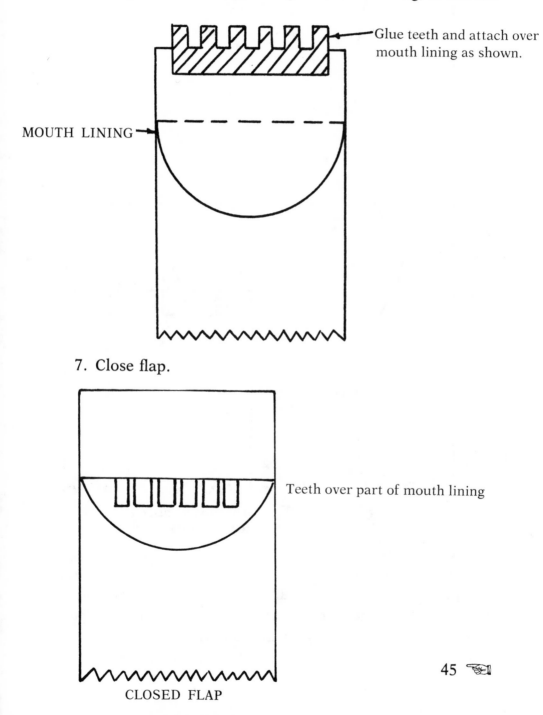

Glue teeth and attach over mouth lining as shown.

MOUTH LINING

7. Close flap.

Teeth over part of mouth lining

CLOSED FLAP

45

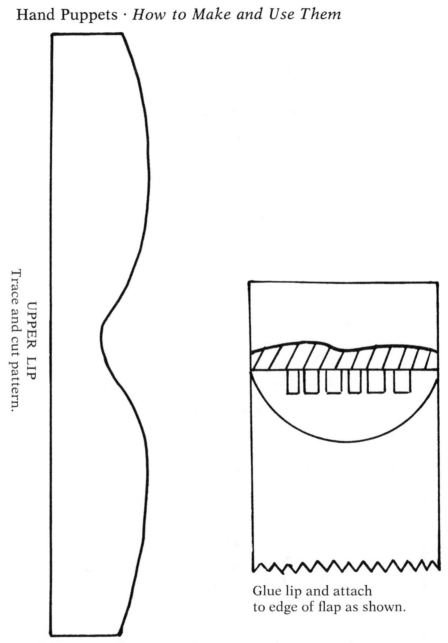

UPPER LIP
Trace and cut pattern.

Glue lip and attach
to edge of flap as shown.

8. For puppet's upper lip, trace diagram. Cut pattern. Pin pattern to red felt. Cut around pattern. Remove pins.
9. Put glue on one side and attach to outer bottom edge of closed flap directly above the teeth, as shown.

10. For puppet's nose, trace diagram. Cut pattern. Pin pattern to green felt. Cut around pattern. Remove pins.

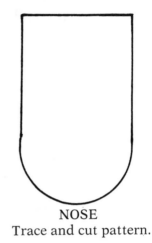

NOSE
Trace and cut pattern.

11. Put glue on one side and attach directly above upper lip at appropriate place, as shown.

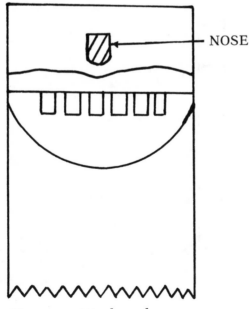

← NOSE

Glue nose. Attach as shown.

12. For puppet's hat, trace diagram and transfer to yellow construction paper. Cut a strip of black construction paper ¼ inch wide and 6¼ inches long. Put glue on one side and attach across lower section of hat for hat band as shown.

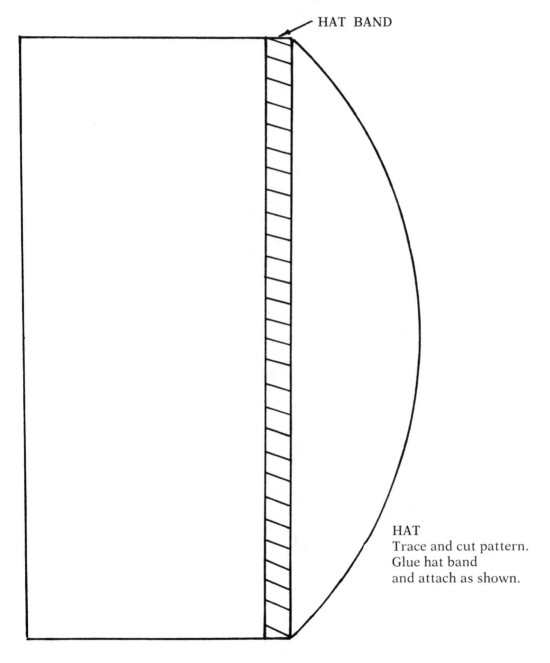

HAT BAND

HAT
Trace and cut pattern.
Glue hat band
and attach as shown.

13. For hat decoration, trace diagram and transfer to black construction paper. Paste on one side and attach to hat as shown (see pages 49 and 50).

HAT DECORATION
Trace and cut pattern.

14. Put glue on the back of visor of hat and attach to flap so that the bottom part barely touches the top of nose.

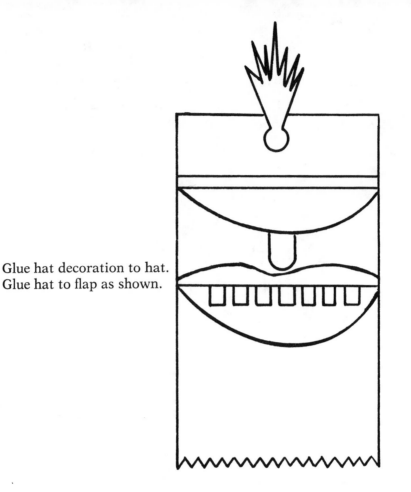

Glue hat decoration to hat.
Glue hat to flap as shown.

15. For puppet's eyes, trace diagram. Cut pattern. Pin pattern on two pieces of black felt. Cut around pattern. Remove pins.

16. For pupils, cut two smaller pieces of blue felt same shape as eyes. Put glue on one side of each and superimpose over center of black felt.

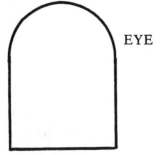

EYE

Trace and cut pattern
on double material.

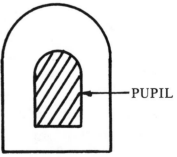

PUPIL

Glue pupil and attach
to eye as shown.

17. Put glue on back of each eye and attach to flap at appropriate place on each side of nose as shown.

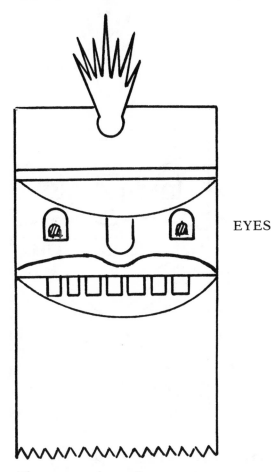

EYES

Glue eyes and attach
to flap as shown.

18. For puppet's shoulder straps, cut two pieces of white construction paper 11 inches long, 1 inch wide.

19. Put glue on one side of each and attach to front of bag from lower corner diagonally across to opposite shoulder point. This will crisscross the messenger's shoulder straps.

20. With scissors, trim the lower and upper corners of straps to edge of bag. Your messenger puppet is now ready to perform.

COMPLETED MESSENGER
PAPER BAG PUPPET

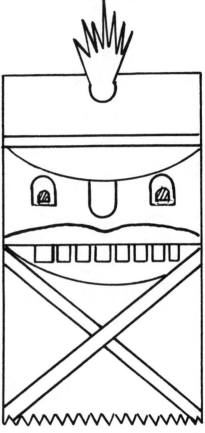

Glue and crisscross
shoulder straps to front of bag.

Directions for Making the King Paper Bag Puppet for Rumpelstiltskin

Materials Needed

Paper bag 6¼ inches by 13¼ inches
String
Paper toweling or newspaper
Cardboard or construction paper
Yellow construction paper

Black, blue, red felt
or construction paper
Elmer's Glue-All or Sobo glue
Black yarn
Scissors
Dowel 10 inches long by ½ inch wide
Wooden base, 3½ inches by 3½ inches
Nail
Hammer
Tracing paper
Pencil
Ruler
Stapler machine

Directions to Follow

1. For puppet stand, nail dowel in center of wooden base as shown.

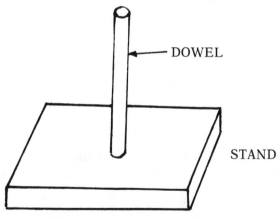

Nail dowel to stand.

2. Draw a rough sketch on paper of what you want the puppet to look like, with some attention to details. Since the king wears a crown, it would be best to make the stuffed paper bag puppet.

3. For puppet's neck, use an empty toilet paper tube. Since the tube is too wide for your finger and the finished puppet's neck, open it by unrolling it flat. Then re-roll it around your index finger for size. Measure it so that you have a tube 4 inches long. Cut off the excess. Tie a string around it.

4. For puppet's head, stuff the bottom flap of the bag with crushed paper toweling or newspaper approximately half the size of the bag.

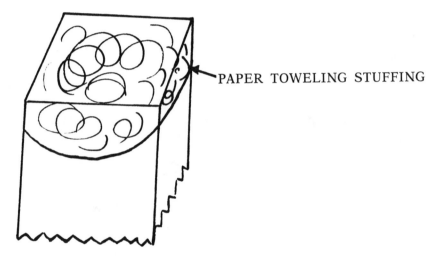

PAPER TOWELING STUFFING

5. Tuck in the corners of the head so as to make the face appear round rather than square.

6. Glue the outside of cylinder and insert it into the center of the stuffed toweling paper so that most of it is in the wad of paper with part below it.

7. Wrap a piece of strong string just below the stuffed head so that a portion of the tube will remain below it. Tie it tightly. You will use this tube to insert your index finger to move the king's head, as shown.

8. For puppet's arms, cut a hole on each side of the bag for your thumb and third finger, as shown. Using your

own fingers for the puppet's **arms** will make it more life-like and you can pick up and hold objects more easily.

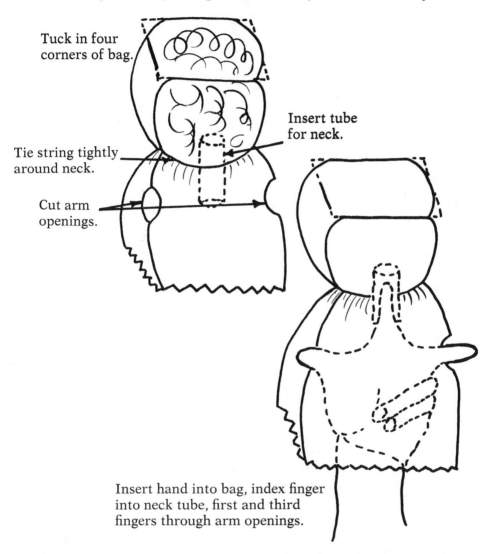

Tuck in four corners of bag.

Insert tube for **neck.**

Tie string tightly around neck.

Cut arm openings.

Insert hand into bag, index finger into neck tube, first and third fingers through arm openings.

9. Place puppet on stand by inserting the top of the dowel into neck of puppet. This will hold the puppet upright as you continue to work with both hands adding the king's features.

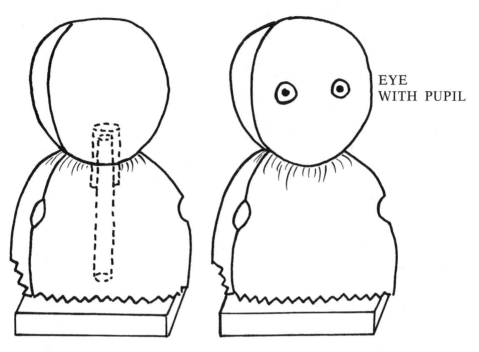

EYE
WITH PUPIL

Place puppet on stand.   Glue eyes over each eye backing.

10. For puppet's eyes, place 2 pieces of black felt together and cut a round circle about 1½ inches wide. Cut 2 smaller pieces of blue felt for pupils and glue over the black felt.

11. Crumple and shape 2 pieces of paper toweling into a ball smaller than the eyes. Glue these pieces of paper to the appropriate place on the puppet's face to form the backing of the eyes.

12. Glue the black felt pieces over each eye backing. The eyes are now raised slightly from the surface of the face.

13. For the puppet's nose, cut a round circle of red felt about ¾ inch wide. Put glue on one side and attach this to appropriate place on face first using a backing, the same as you did for the eyes.

14. For puppet's mouth, trace diagram. Cut pattern. Pin pattern to red felt. Cut around pattern. Remove pins.

MOUTH
Trace and cut pattern.

15. Glue one side and attach under nose as shown, leaving space between for moustache.

16. For puppet's moustache, measure and cut several strands of black yarn 4½ inches long. Bunch together and apply glue at center to hold. Apply to puppet's face between the nose and mouth.

NOSE
MOUTH

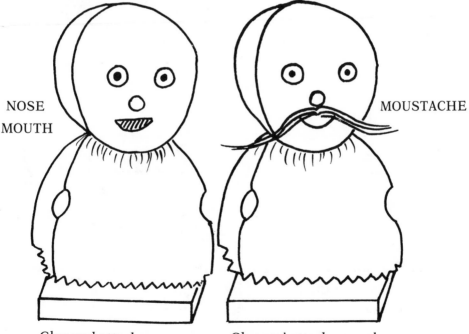

MOUSTACHE

Glue and attach nose and mouth as shown.

Glue and attach several strands of yarn for moustache.

17. For puppet's beard, trace diagram. Cut pattern. Pin pattern to black felt. Cut around pattern. Cut along dotted lines. Remove pins.

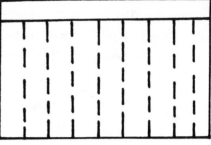

BEARD
Trace and cut pattern. Cut dotted lines.

18. Put glue on one side along top uncut edge and attach under puppet's mouth.

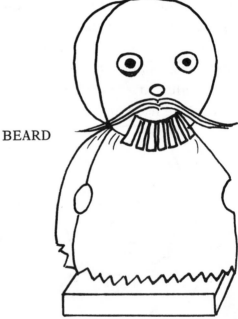

BEARD

Glue beard. Attach as shown.

19. For puppet's crown, measure and cut yellow construction paper 20 inches long by 4½ inches wide.

20. Draw a line 1½ inches from top edge.

21. Measure off 1½ inches along top edge and along drawn line.

22. With a ruler, connect alternating points at edge with points on line.

23. Cut these slits from edge of strip to the line. These slits will be evenly spaced.

CROWN
20 inches long, 4½ inches wide

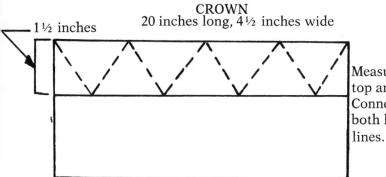

1½ inches

Measure off 1½ inches at top and middle lines. Connect alternating points of both lines. Cut along dotted lines.

24. Fit the crown around puppet's head for size and attach the two sides together with staples or glue.

25. Place the crown over puppet's head. If necessary, use glue here and there to secure to head. The king is now ready to rule the puppet stage!

COMPLETED KING
PAPER BAG PUPPET

CROWN

Directions for Making the Miller's Daughter Paper Bag Puppet for Rumpelstiltskin

Materials Needed

Paper bag 6 ¼ by 13 ¼ inches
String
Toweling paper or newspaper
Cardboard or construction paper
Yellow construction paper
Yellow, blue, and red felt
or construction paper
Scissors
Tracing paper
Pencil
Ruler
Elmer's Glue-All or Sobo glue
Dowel 10 inches long ½ inch wide
Wooden base 3 ½ inches by 3 ½ inches
Nail
Hammer
Stapler machine

Directions to Follow

1. For puppet stand, nail dowel in center of wooden base.

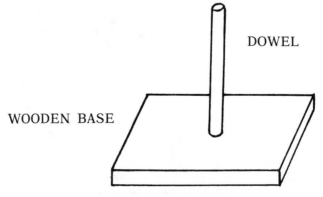

DOWEL

WOODEN BASE

Nail dowel to base.

2. Draw a rough sketch on paper of what you want the puppet to look like, with some attention to details. Since the miller's daughter in *Rumpelstiltskin* will eventually wear a crown, it would be best to construct the stuffed paper bag puppet.

3. For puppet's neck, use an empty toilet paper tube. Since the tube is too wide for your finger and the finished puppet's neck, open it by unrolling it flat. Then re-roll it around your index finger for size. Measure it so that you have a tube 4 inches long. Cut off the excess. Tie a stiing around it.

4. For puppet's head, stuff the bottom flap of the paper bag with crushed paper toweling or newspaper approximately ½ the size of the bag.

5. Tuck in the corners of the head so as to make the face appear round rather than square.

6. Put glue on the outside of the cylinder and insert it into the center of the stuffed paper toweling so that most of it remains in the wad of paper and some below it.

7. Wrap a piece of strong string just below the stuffed head so that a portion of the tube will protrude below it. Tie it tightly. You will use this tube to insert your index finger to move the head.

8. For puppet's arms, cut a hole on each side of the bag for your thumb and third finger. Using your own fingers for the puppet's arms will make it more lifelike and you can pick up and hold objects more easily.

9. Place puppet on stand by inserting the top of the dowel into neck of puppet. This will hold the puppet upright as you continue to work with both hands adding the features.

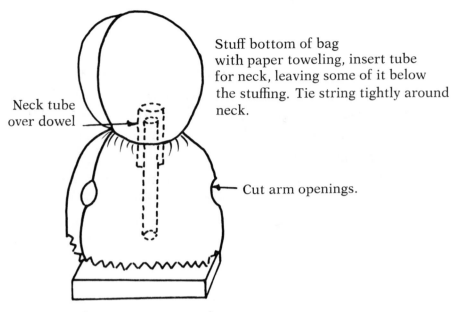

Neck tube over dowel

Stuff bottom of bag with paper toweling, insert tube for neck, leaving some of it below the stuffing. Tie string tightly around neck.

Cut arm openings.

Place puppet on stand.

10. The dimensions for the hair pattern are given on the diagram on page 63. Note that the diagram represents only half the pattern. Draw and cut pattern. Pin pattern on the fold of a *double* piece of yellow felt. Cut around pattern. Cut along dotted lines. Remove pins. Open felt to full size.
11. Apply glue here and there to the uncut center section.
12. Lay felt on puppet's head so that the 12-inch side with the short strands will lie across head from side to side and the short bangs will fall over puppet's forehead. The long strands will fall over the back of the head.
13. For puppet's eyelashes, trace and cut pattern on page 64. Pin it to *double* piece of blue felt. Cut around pattern. Remove pins.
14. Apply glue on one side of upper straight edge of each. Attach to appropriate places on puppet's face.
15. For puppet's nose, cut a small round piece of red felt. Put glue on one side and attach to appropriate place on face between the eyes.

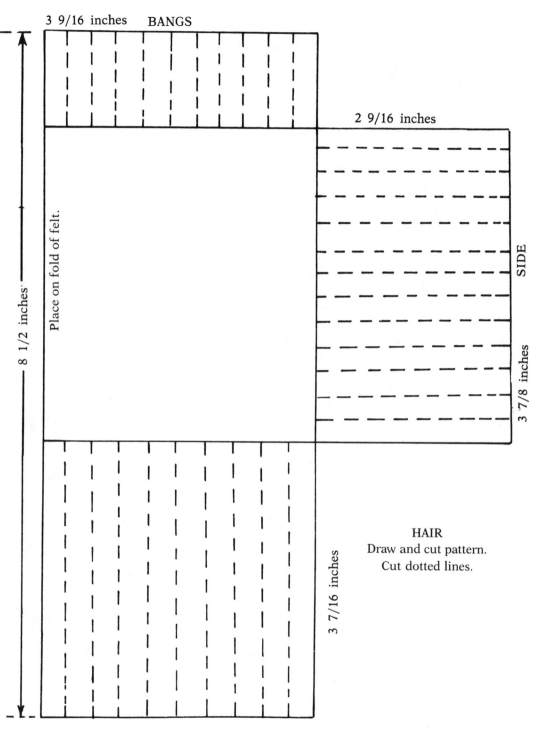

3 9/16 inches BANGS

2 9/16 inches

SIDE

3 7/8 inches

8 1/2 inches

Place on fold of felt.

HAIR
Draw and cut pattern.
Cut dotted lines.

3 7/16 inches

BACK

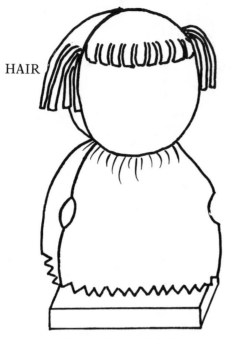

HAIR

Glue and attach hair.

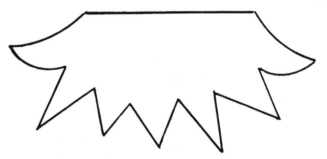

EYELASH
Trace and cut pattern
on double material.

16. For puppet's mouth, trace diagram. Cut pattern. Pin pattern to piece of red felt. Cut around pattern. Cut around dotted lines. Remove pins.

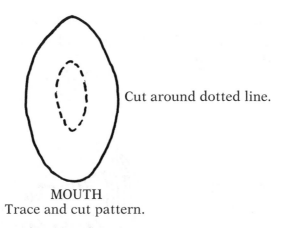

Cut around dotted line.

MOUTH
Trace and cut pattern.

17. Apply glue to one side and attach to appropriate place under the puppet's nose.

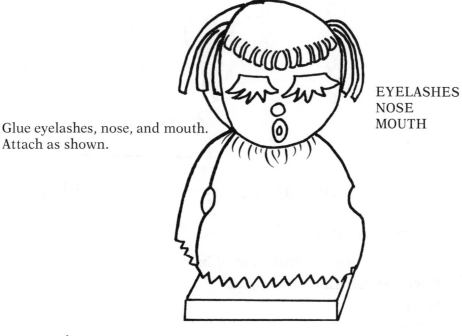

Glue eyelashes, nose, and mouth.
Attach as shown.

EYELASHES
NOSE
MOUTH

18. If you wish, you may attach a piece of decorative ribbon to puppet's hair.

19. When the miller's daughter becomes queen in the

play, attach a crown to her head. See directions for the king puppet, steps 19 to 25, to make and attach crown. The queen is then ready to rule.

CROWN

COMPLETED QUEEN
PAPER BAG PUPPET

Directions for Making a Spinning Wheel Prop

Materials Needed

Heavy cardboard 8 inches by 9 inches
Elmer's Glue-All or Sobo glue
Scissors
Tracing paper
Pencil
Straight pin
Mastic or Scotch Tape

Directions to Follow

1. Trace wheel diagram and draw posts according to dimensions given on page 68. Transfer to heavy cardboard. Cut diagrams and fold or cut at dotted lines as directed on drawing.

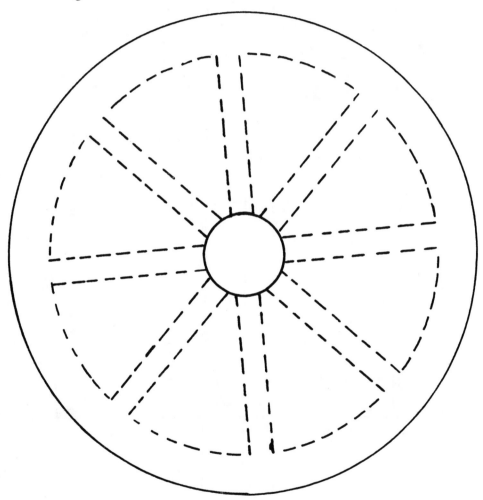

WHEEL FOR SPINNING WHEEL PROP
Trace and cut pattern. Cut along dotted lines.

2. Apply glue to inner top edge of the shorter pole. Attach to the taller pole so that both are balanced upright.

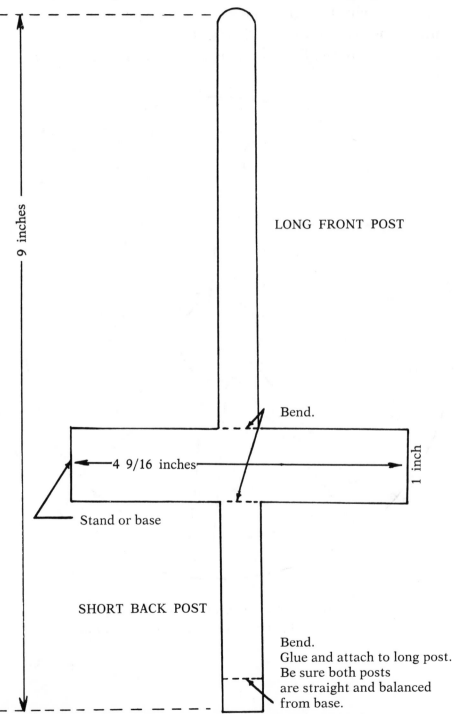

9 inches

LONG FRONT POST

Bend.

4 9/16 inches

1 inch

Stand or base

SHORT BACK POST

Bend.
Glue and attach to long post.
Be sure both posts
are straight and balanced
from base.

3. Apply a small piece of mastic or Scotch Tape to the exterior side of the folds to reinforce them.

4. Insert a straight pin through center of wheel and pierce through the top of the taller pole. The wheel can now be turned around.

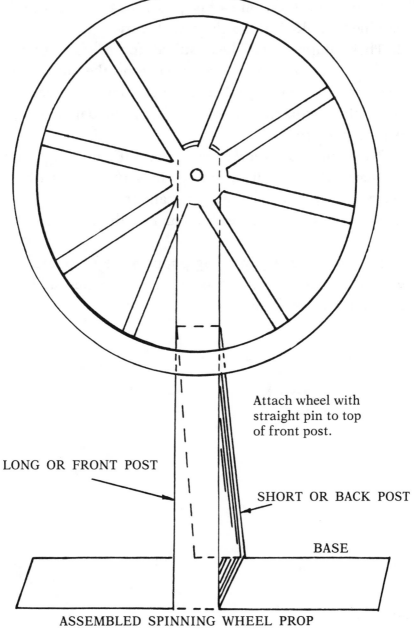

Attach wheel with straight pin to top of front post.

LONG OR FRONT POST

SHORT OR BACK POST

BASE

ASSEMBLED SPINNING WHEEL PROP

Things to Remember in Performing with Paper Bag Puppets

1. Remember these are only paper bag puppets and so very perishable. Handle them with care.
2. These puppets are best suited for a stage that has plenty of room to perform on, such as the simple sheet stage or table-top stage. A floor-length puppet stage, which is usually small, can be too confining for paper bag puppets to perform.
3. They show up very nicely, too, with no stage at all. However, the only disadvantage in performing without a stage of any kind is that you cannot use a script. You must know your story well enough without having to refer to it.
4. Remember that paper bag puppets are more attractive with features of felt or construction paper added on rather than drawn on.

Rod Puppets For A Shadow
{2} Play

Like hand puppets, rod puppets (sometimes called stick puppets) are handled by the puppeteer stationed below the figure. It is an ancient type of puppet, which was and still is very popular in India, China, Egypt, Turkey, and Indonesia. The ancient puppeteer used toughened leather, which was skillfully cut out, hand-tooled, and decorated with color. Today, the rod puppet is gaining favor in our country, especially used as a shadow puppet.

There are different types of rod puppets. The simplest is cut out of cardboard and is a flat outline of a figure. It has a rod attached to the back, which is held by the puppeteer who moves the figure back and forth without moving any part of its body. This type of rod puppet can perform in front of the stage but is best behind a screen as a shadow puppet. If you use it in front of a stage, you may wish to dress it with crepe paper or cloth to achieve a more realistic, round effect. It can also be colored with crayon.

Another type of rod puppet has different parts of the body cut out of cardboard and attached together by means of paper fasteners. A holding rod is placed behind the puppet to hold it upright. A second rod, which moves the puppet, is attached to one of the legs. A network of wires is used on various parts of the puppet's body to move it. This network of wires can be attached to the arms, legs, head, or trunk of a puppet to move these parts.

For example, by attaching a piece of wire to the upper part of the leg onto the corresponding arm, both the leg and arm move up and down when the moving rod is moved up and down. Different arrangements of wire network can be worked out to achieve different kinds of movement. You may wish to move only arms or only legs or both. The first rod is used mainly to hold the puppet upright and the second rod to make it move. This type of puppet can also perform in front of the stage but is best behind a screen as a shadow puppet.

There are also jointed, or movable, rod puppets which have heads made of papier-mâché, dressed and operated by means of a rod in the head. If you wish, this rod can be twirled between thumb and index finger making the head turn right to left. Arms can be made of cloth, cardboard, or even lightweight wood. The arms can be made in two sections and jointed at the shoulders and elbows with paper fasteners, wire, string, or shoelaces. If the joints

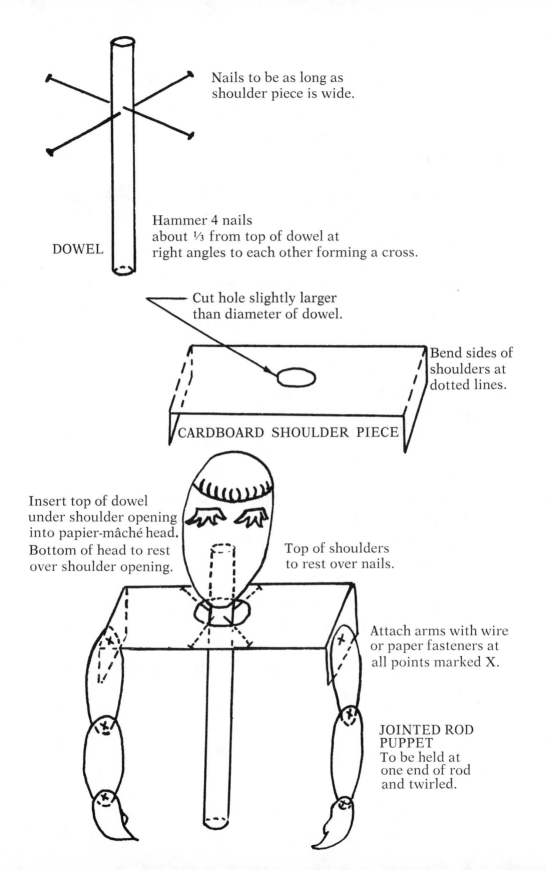

Nails to be as long as
shoulder piece is wide.

DOWEL

Hammer 4 nails
about ⅓ from top of dowel at
right angles to each other forming a cross.

Cut hole slightly larger
than diameter of dowel.

Bend sides of
shoulders at
dotted lines.

CARDBOARD SHOULDER PIECE

Insert top of dowel
under shoulder opening
into papier-mâché head.
Bottom of head to rest
over shoulder opening.

Top of shoulders
to rest over nails.

Attach arms with wire
or paper fasteners at
all points marked X.

**JOINTED ROD
PUPPET**
To be held at
one end of rod
and twirled.

are loosely attached, the arms can swing loosely, somewhat like a jumping jack when the rod is moved vigorously up and down. This type of puppet is best used in front of a stage.

Now I shall explain how to make flat shadow puppets. Shadow puppets are a form of rod puppets, which are not seen by the audience in front of the stage but appear as silhouettes on a white screen. These silhouettes are projected on the screen by a strong light from behind the stage. It is best to draw them in profile view since profile figures are sharp, clear, and recognizable. However, a silhouette puppet can also be drawn with its body in front view and the head in side view.

Making a rod puppet is mainly a problem in drawing. Visualize what your puppet will look like and will be doing before starting. Then draw a small rough sketch showing a specific action.

Since the story and music on record of *Peter and the Wolf* by Prokofiev has a good deal of action, I have chosen this as an example for rod puppets in action poses. The figures in the story have been drawn in sharp profile with the exception of Peter, sitting in the tree in front view with a profile head.

Usually one main action pose is sufficient. However, when necessary have as many as needed to present the story clearly. For example, in *Peter and the Wolf*, it is necessary to show two puppets of Peter, one walking and the other sitting in the tree. The same is true with the wolf—one that shows him slinking around when he first makes his appearance and the other when he gobbles up the duck. The duck also has two figures—one talking to

PETER
Draw and cut outline.

PETER SITTING IN TREE
Trace and cut outline.

the bird (which can also be used when swimming in the pond), and the other fleeing from the wolf.

You can use the same stage as for hand puppets except

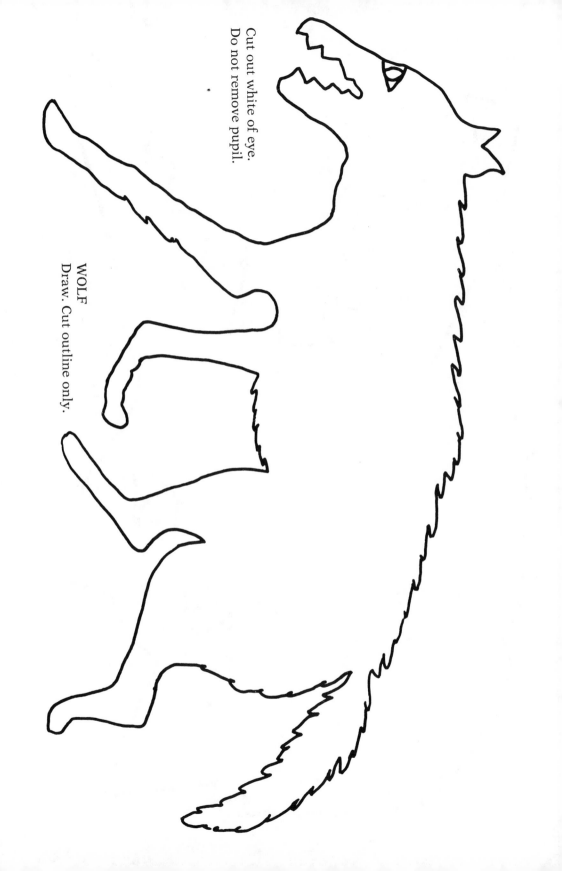

Cut out white of eye.
Do not remove pupil.

WOLF
Draw. Cut outline only.

WOLF
Draw. Cut outline only.

Cut out whites of eyes.
Do not remove pupil.

Cut out white of eye. Do not remove pupil.

DUCK
Draw.
Cut outline only.

Cut out white of eye.
Do not remove pupil.

DUCK
Trace. Cut outline only.

Cut out white of eye.
Do not remove pupil.

BIRD
Trace. Cut outline only.

that a white window shade must be suspended from the top front of the proscenium. Props can easily be attached onto the floor of the stage, behind the screen, with Scotch or mastic tape. The rod puppet is operated from the base of the stage so that the action goes from right to left, and then back again—back and forth behind the screen. When using a puppet stage with a window-shade attachment, be sure you have one with a shelf underneath which can hold the puppets to be used.

A white window shade or movie-projector screen can also be attached to the frame of an open doorway. When using either, be sure to have a table underneath as a stage.

Pull the screen down over the open doorway with the audience sitting on one side and the puppeteer on the other. The open doorway will allow the light behind you to pass through the shade. The table top is used for props which are cut in outline form and attached to it with Scotch or mastic tape. The size of the shade is determined by the width of the doorway.

Use a strong light like that of a slide projector, which is placed above and behind you on a shelf. Be sure that the light does not shine directly at your head since this will cause an outline of your head to be projected onto the screen. Sit or kneel below the direct source of light, which must shine directly onto the screen. Hold the rods above your head right in front of the beam of light. Your rod puppets, which are held between the screen and the light, will appear to the audience on the opposite side as silhouettes. The closer the puppets are held to the screen, the smaller and sharper they will appear to the audience; the farther away from the screen, the larger and less distinct.

Hold the rod puppets so that as little of the rod is shown on the screen as possible. Move the puppets from right to left on the screen, then turn them around and come back again. Do this in such a manner that their feet are on the floor of the stage if a hand puppet stage is used and on the table if a table and screen are used. However, if some of the rod is shown, the audience will not pay much attention to it. The spectators will concentrate their attention mostly on the puppets themselves, their movement, speech, and music.

In *Peter and the Wolf*, guide your rod puppets from one

HUNTER
Draw. Cut outline.
Note: Cut as many hunters as desired.

HUNTER
Trace and cut outline.
Note: Cut out as many hunters as desired.

side of the screen to the other keeping in time with the music. When you reach the right or left edge of the screen, simply turn your rod puppet around and go back. You can operate one rod puppet in each hand at one time. If and when it is necessary, change from one figure to another or from one position to another at the appropriate place

CAT SITTING IN TREE
Trace and cut outline.

in the narration when the story calls for it. Also, use as many puppeteers as needed for characters to give continuity to the story. Do what the narrator in the story tells you to do. In marching your puppet, tilt the rod slightly forward and up. This will give the impression that the puppet is marching or walking. Remember that when your

85

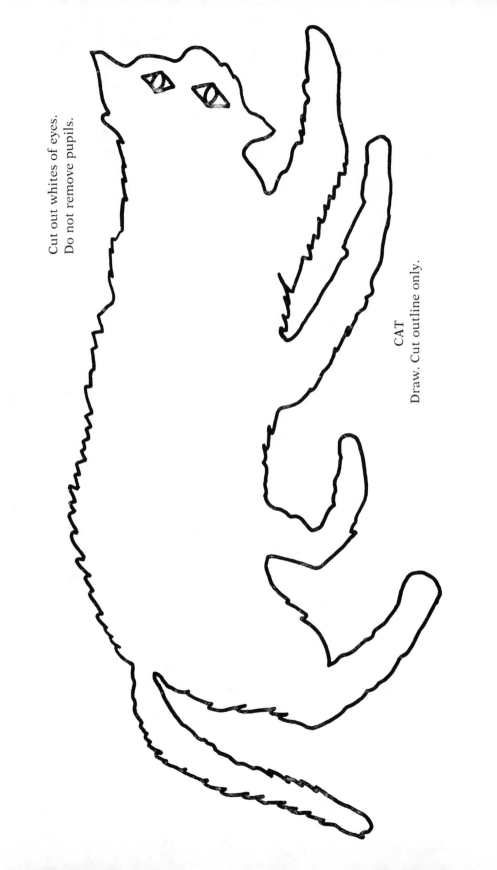

Cut out whites of eyes.
Do not remove pupils.

CAT
Draw. Cut outline only.

puppet is on your right-hand side of the screen, it appears on the left of the screen to the audience sitting on the opposite side, and vice versa.

Since rod puppets have limited movement, do not expect too much action from them. Movements will be slow, but this can be an asset. This type of puppet can be used in a puppet show that requires simple, deliberate movements of mechanical repetition such as marching, walking, dueling, and dancing. You will notice that in *Peter and the Wolf*, all figures show simple action such as walking, flying, slinking, pulling, and marching. Also, since the puppets are easily manipulated, you can better concentrate your attention on the dialogue.

Careful selection of the play must be made where there is simple dialogue and action. Music can also play an important part in the whole production as in *Peter and the Wolf*. A long involved story will have no value on the shadow screen.

Directions for Making Flat Rod Puppets for Peter and the Wolf

Materials Needed

Stiff cardboard paper
Tracing paper
Pencil
Scissors, preferably short, pointed manicure scissors
Rods, ¼" wide, 12" long. One rod to be 18" long
Elmer's Glue-All or Sobo glue
Mastic tape to attach property

Directions to Follow

1. Trace the drawings on pages 76, 80, 81, 84, and 85. The working drawings shown on pages 75, 77, 78, 79, 83, and 86 should be larger. Therefore, trace them and enlarge the finished design.
2. Cut each outline.
3. Glue one end of 12″ rod to the back of each figure as low as possible.
4. Glue the 18″ rod to the back of the bird. This should be longer to enable the bird to fly through the air above the other figures.
5. For prop of tree, enlarge the drawing shown or design your own tree.
6. Bend along dotted line.
7. Attach to floor of stage with mastic tape along fold.

Directions for Making Grandfather Jointed Rod Puppet for Peter and the Wolf

Materials Needed

Stiff cardboard
Two pieces of thin but rigid wire—4½″ long, 10½″ long
Two rods—¼″ wide, 12″ long
Six paper fasteners
Elmer's Glue-All or Sobo glue
Tracing paper
Pencil
Scissors, preferably a short manicure scissors which is excellent for cutting in and out of very small areas

Directions to Follow

1. Trace all parts of the figure on pages 90 and 91 onto stiff cardboard. See directions for tracing in front of book.

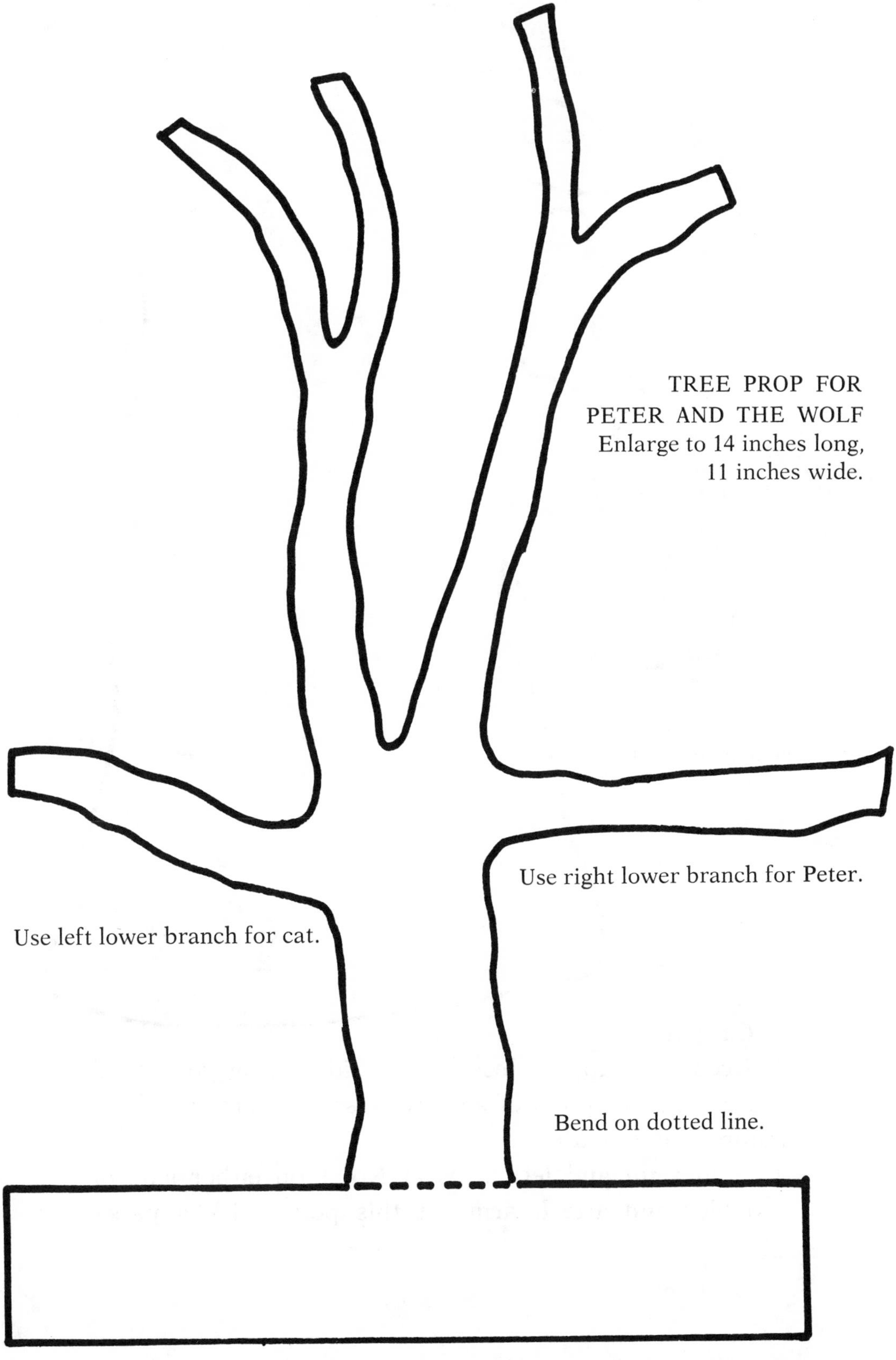

TREE PROP FOR
PETER AND THE WOLF
Enlarge to 14 inches long,
11 inches wide.

Use right lower branch for Peter.

Use left lower branch for cat.

Bend on dotted line.

BODY FOR GRANDFATHER

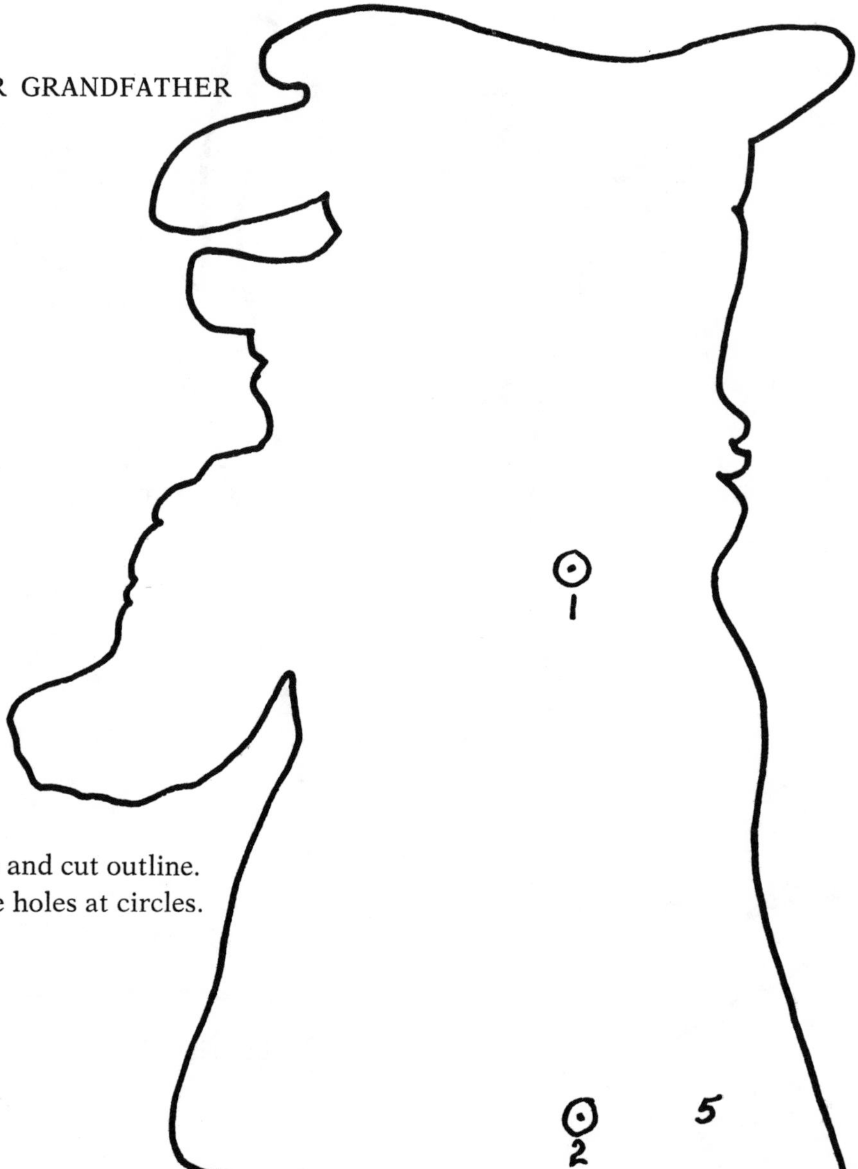

Trace and cut outline.
Pierce holes at circles.

φ
1

φ
2

5

2. Cut pattern.
3. Keep the puppet pieces' front side facing you at all times. With the point of a sharp scissors, pierce a hole at numbers 1, 2, 3, and 4.
4. Hold right and left arms at No. 1 on either side of shoulder and attach arms at this point with a paper

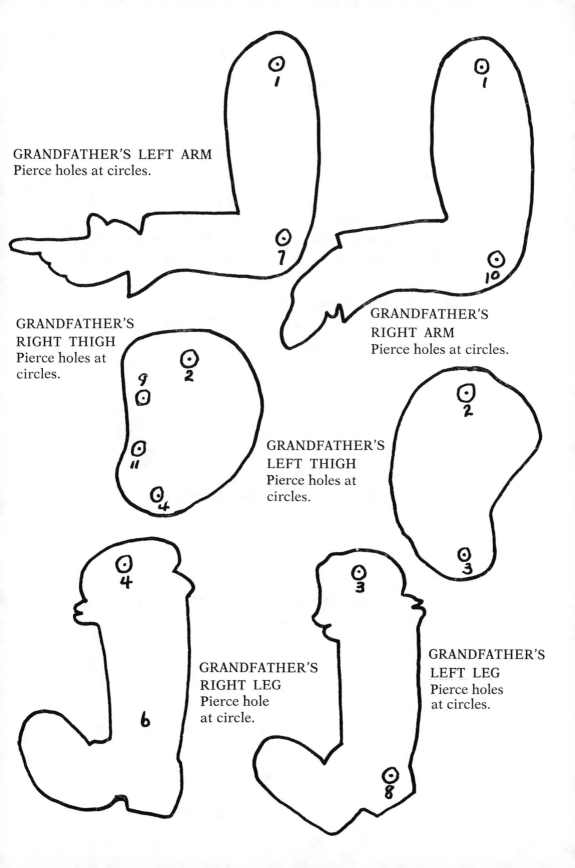

GRANDFATHER'S LEFT ARM
Pierce holes at circles.

GRANDFATHER'S
RIGHT ARM
Pierce holes at circles.

GRANDFATHER'S
RIGHT THIGH
Pierce holes at
circles.

GRANDFATHER'S
LEFT THIGH
Pierce holes at
circles.

GRANDFATHER'S
RIGHT LEG
Pierce hole
at circle.

GRANDFATHER'S
LEFT LEG
Pierce holes
at circles.

fastener. Head of paper fasteners are always to be facing you.

5. Hold right and left thigh over each side of hip at No. 2.

6. Attach thighs at this point with a paper fastener.

7. Attach right and left leg separately over each knee at points No. 3 and No. 4 in the same manner with heads of fasteners facing you.

8. Glue one end of rod at No. 5 (where there is no hole) behind the puppet's body. This becomes the support rod with which the puppet is held upright.

9. Glue end of another rod at No. 6 (where there is no hole) behind the puppet's right leg. This becomes the control rod which will move the puppet.

10. With the point of a scissors, pierce a hole at Nos. 7, 8, 9, 10, and 11.

11. Place puppet in following position facing you: Right arm up (saluting), right leg up at right angle position (marching). Keep left arm at waist level and left leg straight down.

12. With a piece of wire 4½" long, pass one end through No. 11 from back to front and hook this end over thigh to hold.

13. Pass other end of same wire through No. 10 from front to back and hook it over arm to hold.

14. Keep puppet in same position. With another piece of wire 10½" long, pass one end from front to back at No. 9. Hook it over thigh to hold.

15. Pass the other end of the same wire from back to front through No. 7 and bend it over elbow to hold.

16. Keeping the puppet in same position, pass the end of same wire down to No. 8 through the back and hook this end over left leg to hold. See diagram.

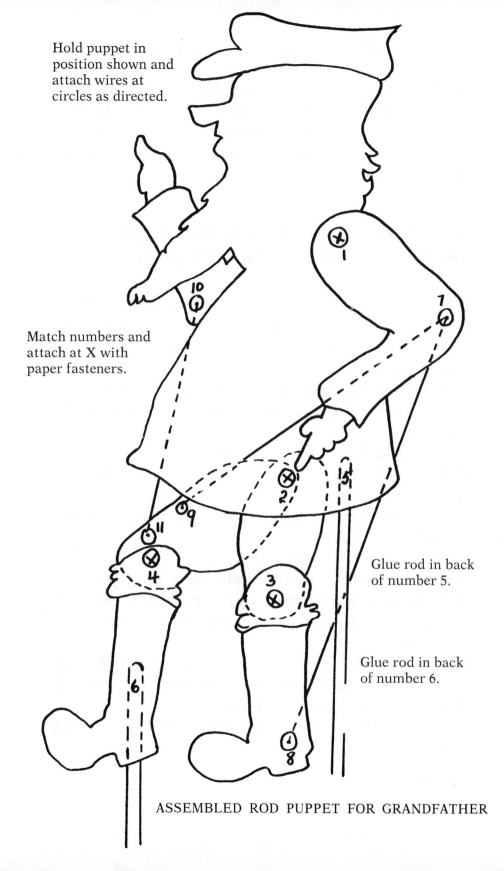

Hold puppet in position shown and attach wires at circles as directed.

Match numbers and attach at X with paper fasteners.

Glue rod in back of number 5.

Glue rod in back of number 6.

ASSEMBLED ROD PUPPET FOR GRANDFATHER

17. Turn the puppet with its back facing you. Hold puppet with holding rod in left hand and move rod up and down. Now grandfather walks and moves his arms.

Experiment and think of ways to make your puppet move differently by means of a network of wires.

Things to Remember in Performing the Shadow Play of Peter and the Wolf

1. Listen to the record of *Peter and the Wolf* music by Prokofiev over and over again. Become familiar with the story so as to know when to switch puppets and what movements to use.
2. Use a white screen or window shade attached across a door opening or else a puppet stage with a screen attachment.
3. Place a table behind the screen if a doorway is used.
4. Spread out the stick puppets on the table for easy reach.
5. Place three chairs behind the table for three puppeteers.
6. If a doorway is used, place a projector several feet behind the screen above the head level of the puppeteers. If a puppet stage, use flood lights attached to the inner corners of the back stage. See illustration of completed floor stage.
7. Place a record player behind the screen within easy reach of the puppeteers or stagehand. Place the record of *Peter and the Wolf* on record player.
8. Place the loudspeaker in front of the screen facing the audience.

9. Arrange the viewers' chairs in rows about six feet from the screen.

10. Pull all window shades down.

11. Turn overhead lights out and projector light on.

12. Stagehand or one puppeteer starts the record player.

13. Listen carefully to the narrator and the music. When the narrator tells about a character, pick it up quickly by the end of the rod from the table before you. The narrator will tell whether to make your stick puppets walk, creep, waddle, or fly. The music will be very suggestive of the rhythm and will tell you whether to move quickly or slowly.

14. In moving the puppets, be sure not to make them bump into one another. This is achieved by holding the puppet in one hand a little before or behind the other.

Papier-Mâché
{3} Puppets

There is nothing mysterious or difficult in making papier-mâché puppets.

Papier-mâché is simply paper dipped in a paste solution and molded with the fingers into a form. When allowed to dry it becomes stiff and hard and very lightweight.

The paste solution can be made with ordinary baking flour poured gradually into a bowl of cold water and stirred into a creamy thickness.

The best paste solution is made with a powdered wallpaper glue which is poured gradually into cold water and stirred until it becomes thick as cream.

Make a fresh batch of paste each time you start working with paper. Do not leave it standing overnight or it will dry up.

The basic paper used is ordinary newspaper or paper toweling. However, do not hesitate to experiment with paper from a discarded telephone directory, brown wrapping paper or any other kind of paper. I prefer to use paper toweling because it is soft and easy to handle.

All paper has a grain which tears easily. Find out which side has this grain by tearing off a narrow strip. Tearing *with* the grain of the paper allows you to tear evenly and easily all the way down. Tearing against the grain will tear unevenly and with difficulty.

Always tear *with* the grain. The tear will result in small ragged edges which are good for molding a papier-mâché puppet. These ragged edges will interlock with those of other strips when molding, resulting in an even surface finish. Never use scissors. Strips that are cut with scissors will not interlock with each other and will leave sharp edges on the surface.

Your puppet will be interesting if you give him a definite personality. He should have his own particular characteristics unlike any other one. Exaggerate at least one feature so that one puppet can be distinguished from another. This can be done by giving him an extra big nose, a crooked mouth or large eyes and ears.

Also exaggerate when it has a bearing on the story. For example, we will make our Punch and Judy with large noses, chins, and eyes because in the play, Punch refers to his beautiful nose and to Judy's beauty. He knows perfectly well that this is not true but he pretends it is so. He is spoofing all along and we show this by exaggerating his and Judy's appearance.

Punch

Since your puppets do not actually move their mouths to speak, it is a good idea to construct them with open mouths to create an illusion of talking.

A puppet that will be required to look sad one minute and happy the next must not be made with a wide grin or a miserable expression. Create this type of puppet with a calm expression.

As one professional puppeteer has said, a puppet is not a doll, but rather an actor. Therefore, do not concentrate on small details, but on the big things such as eyes, nose, and mouth. Again, exaggerate for effect if necessary. Never sandpaper the puppet's face for smoothness, but rather, allow it to retain the rough textural quality of the paper. The lights of the stage will play on the rough surface creating dark and light shadows. These in turn will add realism to the puppet's features.

For this reason also, do not overdress a puppet. The costume must be simple and bold and designed for an audience which will be seeing the puppet from a distance.

Plain fabrics are best, except when a design in the fabric adds to the characteristic of the puppet as, for example, in *Punch and Judy*. A black polka-dot fabric for Punch is excellent since he is so clownish. A calico dress and gingham apron for Judy, since she is a housewife, are good.

The characters in the old play, *Punch and Judy*, lend themselves best to papier-mâché technique. They can be made in so many different ways, can be dressed according to character, and can be moved to show almost all kinds of action.

In creating these papier-mâché puppets, be daring and inventive and you will be rewarded with puppets that are unique.

99

The Doctor

Papier-Mâché Technique for Punch-and-Judy Puppets

Materials Needed

Newspaper or paper toweling
Powdered wallpaper glue
Bowl
Tablespoon
Scotch tape or string
Cardboard
Dowel 10″ long, ½″ wide
3½″ x 3½″ wooden base
Hammer and nail
Brush
Tempera paints—white, red, yellow, blue, black
Scissors
Nail file

Directions to Follow

1. Spread newspaper on table to work on.
2. For puppet stand, nail dowel in center of wooden base.

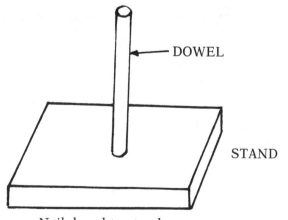

— DOWEL

STAND

Nail dowel to stand.

101

3. For puppet's neck, use an empty toilet paper tube. Since the tube is too wide for your finger and the finished puppet's neck, open it by unrolling it flat. Then re-roll it around your index finger for size. Measure it so that you have a tube 4 inches long. Cut off the excess. Tie a string around it.

4. For the foundation of the head, crumble some paper toweling into the shape you will want the finished product to be. Oval if the head is to be oval shaped, long if the head is to be long, round or square if the head is to be round or square. This basic form is the most important part of constructing papier-mâché puppets. It determines what your finished puppet will look like since the rest is simply building upon it. Build the foundation a little bit larger than the size of the finished puppet since it will shrink in the process of drying.

LONG SHAPE   ROUND SHAPE   SQUARE SHAPE

5. Tie the foundation with a piece of string or Scotch Tape it so that the shape will hold.

6. Mix the paste by gradually pouring the powdered wallpaper glue into a bowl of cold water, stirring constantly with a tablespoon to a creamy consistency. Be sure all lumps are eliminated.

7. For the puppet's neck, make a hole with a pencil or the

point of scissors at the base of the foundation. Make it large enough for the cardboard cylinder to fit into it. Pour a little of the glue into the hole. Cover the outer side of the cylinder with glue and insert it into the hole with a screwing motion so that it fits snugly into the head. Allow a small portion of it to protrude from the bottom. This will become the puppet's visible neck.

8. Cover the shaped foundation with a layer of glue. This will help to hold the basic form together and will also serve as a base on which overlapping strips will be attached.

9. Place the form onto the stand by slipping the cylinder end over the top of the dowel. The stand will hold the form and allow you to use both hands to mold and shape the puppet's head. Turn the stand around as needed to work on all parts of the head.

10. Tear the paper toweling into strips about ¾″ wide with the grain of the paper.

11. Dip these strips one at a time into the paste mixture. Drag each piece over the edge of the bowl to remove excess paste. Be sure that both sides of the strip are covered with paste.

12. Drape these strips over the foundation form one at a time. Each time you place a strip over the foundation, press down with your fingers from the middle outward. This will remove any air pockets, lumps of paste, or excess paste. In this way, the finished puppet will be firmer and more durable.

13. Gradually cover the entire head, making sure the strips overlap at all places. Add layer upon layer, shaping as you go along (see page 104).

14. Allow to stand and dry overnight in a warm room or

Strips of paper toweling
draped over foundation

over a radiator. This drying process is repeated several times during the formation of the head. Papier-mâché must dry from the inside out to be firm and durable.

15. Add more layers of strips, molding and shaping with your fingers as you go along, the same as you would with clay. When necessary, add little wads of paper that have been torn, crumbled up, and soaked in paste. These are to be properly positioned for cheeks, nose, mouth, eyes, eyelids, ears, and so on. Always cover these wads over with pasted strips to anchor onto the face as you would place a bandage over facial features.

16. Remember, puppets are charming when features are exaggerated—such as a large nose, big ears, pointed chin, or high cheekbones. For final shaping, use the round end of a nail file to form the details of these features.

17. Allow to stand and dry overnight or as long as necessary. You will notice that with each drying process, the puppet's head will shrink a little. Build it up as you go along to a desired size. You will also notice that after each drying process it will be easier to work with the head since it will be less slippery.

18. Hair can be created in a number of ways. Invent your

own method. You may choose to shred pieces of Kleenex into a bowl of paste and apply as desired. This makes for nice curly hair. Or, strips of paper toweling dipped in paste can be braided for pigtails. Curls can be twisted strips of paste-saturated paper toweling. Waves can be made with shredded tissue paper saturated in paste and pushed into various wavy shapes on the head.

19. When the desired puppet head is completed, allow to dry thoroughly for as long as necessary. A good test is when the head becomes almost as hard as wood.

20. Paint with poster or tempera paints, mixing colors to a desired shade. Mix the paints with a little water in a cup. White with a touch of red for a lady's light pink flesh tone. To this add a little yellow for a man's darker tone. For different shades of brown, mix red, yellow, and blue, a little at a time until the desired tone is achieved. Experiment with underpainting, which is one color superimposed over another, right on the puppet's head, for textural quality.

21. Allow paint to dry thoroughly.

22. Apply a second coat of paint if you find that the first has dried to a lighter color than desired.

23. Use white for eyes. Allow to dry thoroughly before applying blue or black or brown for the pupils of eyes. A bright red for lips will be attractive when viewing the puppet from a distance. Black for hair or a mixture of red, yellow, and blue for a nice shade of brown. With only your primary colors, red, blue, and yellow you can achieve a number of colors and shades depending on how much of each color is used. Toning it down with a little white is sometimes desirable.

24. Allow paint to dry thoroughly.

105

25. For hardness and durability, apply clear shellac with a small brush over the whole head. The shellac will also make the colors brighter.

26. After the shellac is thoroughly dry, you may want to use strands of colored yarn for hair in place of the papier-mâché hair as described in step 18. Now is the time to paste it on strand by strand using the same wallpaper glue or any good grade of glue.

By applying yarn strand by strand, you can achieve many different effects such as Dutch boy with bangs, shaggy for clown, stylized barber's haircut, swirled up or hanging down or short wavy hair for a girl. Experiment, and see how many styles you can create with this method.

Your puppet is now completed.

Costuming and Dressing the Hand Puppet

Try to think of ways of dressing your puppet to suit its character. For example, a scarecrow should have a torn ragged costume with patches; a clown's clothing should be baggy and covered with large polka dots; a princess should wear pretty silk fabric as well as a crown; a king, queen, and prince should be dressed in clothing of purple, red, or blue velvet and also have crowns; a rich merchant should be costumed in taffeta or other rich-looking cloth. Choose the fabric and color that will add to the personality of your puppet.

Keep your costume simple, with as little trimming as possible. Remember, as has been said, these are actors to be viewed from a distance and not dressed-up dolls for close inspection. Let the print of the fabric, or its solid color, play a major part in costuming. However, if necessary to stress the character of the puppet, you may want to use buttons, rick-rack, lace, ribbons, feathers, sequins, braiding, or scraps of material or felt to trim with. I have used buttons on the policeman for the Punch-and-Judy play because buttons belong on a policeman's uniform.

Punch is costumed in baggy black polka-dotted fabric because he is a clown. Attach a stick to his hand, which could be a pencil painted black. Judy, being a housewife, is costumed in calico print, with a checked apron and a dust cap on her head. The baby wears white with a fancy white-lace cap. Scaramouch, being an artist, wears a blue smock and beret. The doctor, of course, wears a white smock. The policeman wears a navy-blue costume with a white badge, and brass or navy buttons sewn on it. He also carries a stick to smack Punch with. The devil has a costume of fiery red. The hangman wears a black smock and a black mask. Toby, the dog, has a simple brown costume.

Directions for Making a Cloth Costume

Materials Needed

Tracing paper
Pencil
Scissors
Straight pins
Needle and thread if costume is to be sewn
Stapler and staples if costume is to be stapled instead of sewn
Fabric

107

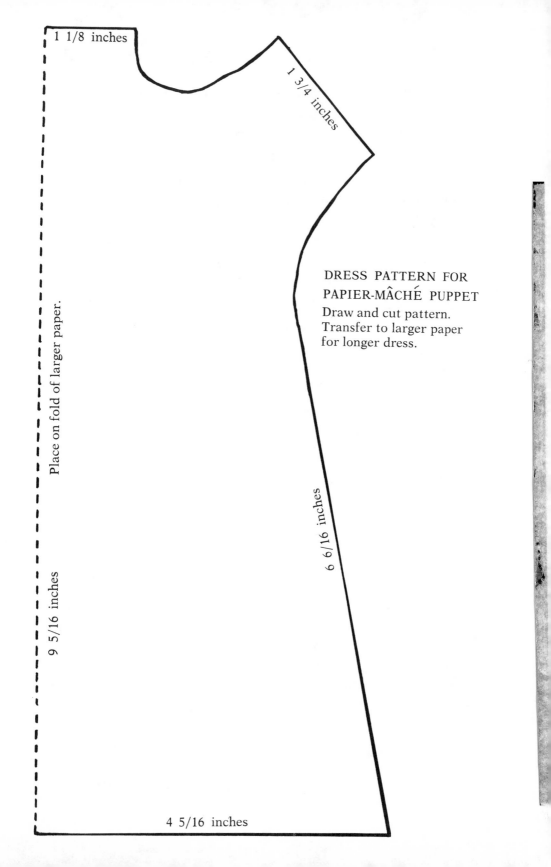

1 1/8 inches

1 3/4 inches

Place on fold of larger paper.

DRESS PATTERN FOR
PAPIER-MÂCHÉ PUPPET
Draw and cut pattern.
Transfer to larger paper
for longer dress.

6 6/16 inches

9 5/16 inches

4 5/16 inches

Directions for Making Costume

1. Draw and cut the pattern according to the dimensions given on page 108. Notice that it is only one half of full size. Fold a large piece of paper in half lengthwise. Lay the cut half of pattern on the folded piece of paper so that the dotted line matches the folded line of paper beneath. Trace and cut the new pattern 2 inches longer. Open new pattern to correct size.

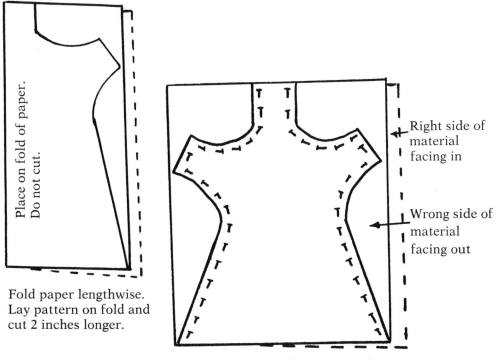

Place on fold of paper.
Do not cut.

Fold paper lengthwise.
Lay pattern on fold and
cut 2 inches longer.

Right side of material facing in

Wrong side of material facing out

Pin pattern on double piece of material and cut around it.

2. Double material, right side in, wrong side out.
3. Lay pattern on material and pin around.

4. Cut material along pattern. If you wish, you may cut the material longer and wider.

5. Remove pins and pattern. Open the two halves.

6. Turn in each sleeve opening on wrong side ¼ inch from edge and baste.

7. Turn in the neck opening of each half on wrong side ¼ inch and baste.

8. Turn in hem of each half on wrong side ¼ inch and baste.

9. Sew sleeve openings, neck openings, and hem openings with small running stitches.

10. Remove basting of each.

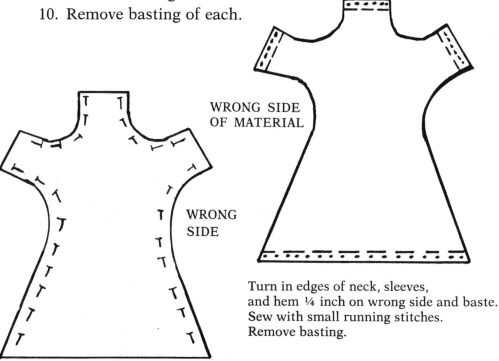

WRONG SIDE
OF MATERIAL

WRONG
SIDE

Turn in edges of neck, sleeves,
and hem ¼ inch on wrong side and baste.
Sew with small running stitches.
Remove basting.

Pin front and back together along shoulders and down sides,
keeping right side facing in, wrong side out.

11. Pin front and back together along shoulders and down sides keeping right side in, wrong side out.

12. Baste together the front and back of costume with needle and thread. Baste ¼ inch from edges of neck and shoulders. Baste along each underarm and sides ¼ inch from edges.

13. Remove pins.

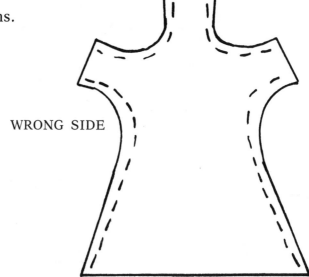

WRONG SIDE

Baste front and back together ¼ inch from edges of neck and shoulders. Baste also along each underarm. Remove pins.

14. Sew the sides along the basting with small running stitches or staple together instead.

15. Remove basting stitches.

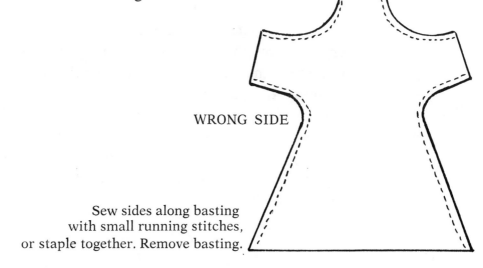

WRONG SIDE

Sew sides along basting with small running stitches, or staple together. Remove basting.

16. Turn costume inside out. Now the right side of fabric is on the outside.

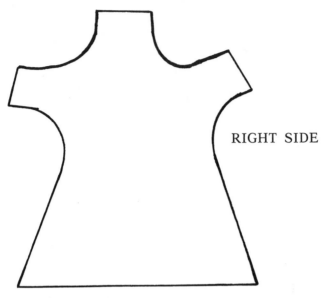

RIGHT SIDE

Turn costume inside out.

17. If the costume is to be a removable one (to be used later on other puppets) try the neck opening on the puppet for size, by slipping it over the puppet's head. If the opening is too large, sew as many tucks around it as necessary to make it smaller and fit snugly.

18. Fit it over the puppet's neck again. Use a rubber band slipped over the puppet's head and onto the neck, over and over as many times as necessary to attach the costume to the puppet securely.

19. If the costume is to be a permanent one for the puppet, simply apply Elmer's glue around the inner wall of the cylinder (puppet's neck) and insert the neck of the costume into it. Be sure your index finger fits into the opening. Allow to dry.

Directions for Making Gallows Prop for Punch-and-Judy Show

Materials Needed

Heavy cardboard 8 inches by 9 inches
Elmer's Glue-All or Sobo glue
Scissors
Tracing paper
Pencil
Mastic or Scotch Tape
Strong cord about 17½ inches long

Directions to Follow (diagrams are on pages 114 and 115)

1. Trace diagrams and transfer to heavy cardboard (see Directions for Tracing, 1 to 13, in front of book). Cut diagrams and fold on dotted lines as directed on drawings.
2. Apply glue to the under section of No. 1 fold and superimpose it over dotted lines on base of gallows.
3. Apply glue to top section of both poles so that the two will hold together and are balanced.
4. Apply glue underneath the No. 2 fold and superimpose it over the No. 3 fold.
5. Apply glue at No. 4 fold so that it will be attached to the under part of the top rod.
6. Apply glue to the underneath base of these attached rods and attach to top of one side of either pole.
7. With the point of the scissors, pierce a hole through the unattached end of the double rods, large enough to pass the cord through.
8. For noose, tie a loop at one end of cord. Pass the other end through without pulling it tight. This makes a free loop.

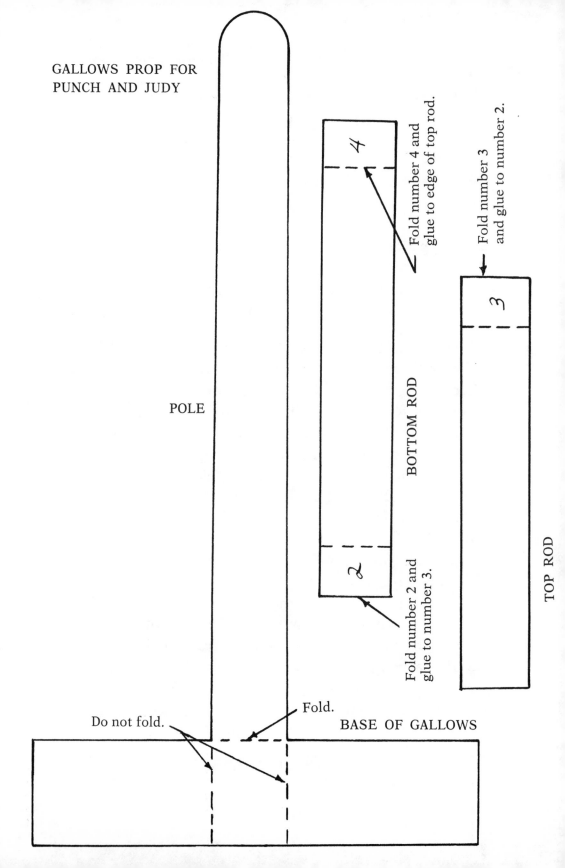

GALLOWS PROP FOR PUNCH AND JUDY

Fold number 4 and glue to edge of top rod.

Fold number 3 and glue to number 2.

4

3

POLE

BOTTOM ROD

TOP ROD

Fold number 2 and glue to number 3.

2

Do not fold.

Fold.

BASE OF GALLOWS

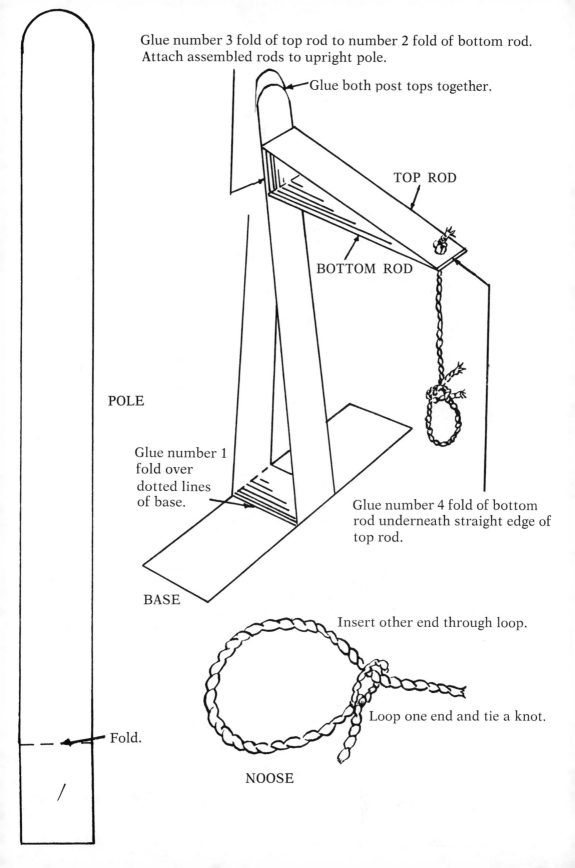

Glue number 3 fold of top rod to number 2 fold of bottom rod.
Attach assembled rods to upright pole.

Glue both post tops together.

TOP ROD

BOTTOM ROD

POLE

Glue number 1
fold over
dotted lines
of base.

Glue number 4 fold of bottom
rod underneath straight edge of
top rod.

BASE

Insert other end through loop.

Loop one end and tie a knot.

Fold.

NOOSE

9. Pass the free end of cord under and through the hole at the unattached end of the double rods.
10. Secure by tying a knot at this end.

Holding the Papier-Mâché Puppet for Action

Placement of Hand in Puppet

1. Place your hand inside the puppet's costume.
2. Place your index finger up through the neck tube and inside the head.
3. Insert thumb in one sleeve and middle finger in other sleeve.
4. Your thumb and middle fingers will become the puppet's arms and hands. Move your thumb and middle finger to make the puppet's arms and hands move, wave, clap,

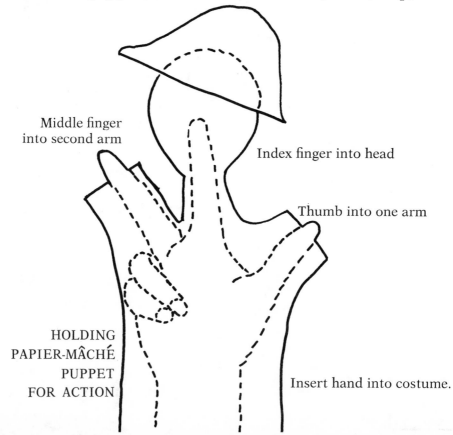

Middle finger
into second arm

Index finger into head

Thumb into one arm

HOLDING
PAPIER-MÂCHÉ
PUPPET
FOR ACTION

Insert hand into costume.

and even pick up objects and hold them. Use your index finger to move the head forward, backward, sideways. Bend your wrist to make your puppet bow and walk.

5. Practice your motions looking at the puppet or watching it in a mirror to see how the movements will appear to the audience.

Things to Remember in Making Papier-Mâché Puppets

1. Pour and stir powder paste into a bowl of water making sure that all lumps are eliminated.

2. Never cut strips of paper—tear instead. But be sure to tear with the grain of the paper.

3. The basic shape of the paper foundation will determine the final shape of the papier-mâché puppet.

4. Exaggerate the puppet's features for identity and also when it has a bearing on the story.

5. Remember that a papier-mâché puppet must be allowed to dry at intervals. Also, in the process of drying, the puppet will shrink to a smaller size, depending on how much water you use in the paste mixture. Allow for this shrinkage in working out the final size of the puppet.

6. In painting the puppet, allow it to dry thoroughly before applying clear shellac.

7. Using your own fingers as the puppet's hands will make it easier for the puppet to perform many movements, such as clapping, waving, and picking up objects.

8. Be as inventive as you like. There is no rule that says that you must follow the directions as laid out in this book. If you can think of a better way, use it.

Creating The
{4} Play

There are ready-made puppet plays that are suitable for a puppet show, some of which you will find in the list of *Some Other Useful Books* on page 189. But be aware that not all ready-made puppet plays you may see are suitable for a fine puppet show. It is lots more fun to write your own play.

A puppet play can be created in two ways. One is to make the puppets first and then write the play suggested by the puppets—the play or story to suit the character of the puppet.

The other is to write the play and then make the puppets to suit the story. It is easier and safer to use this second method for it is less apt to produce a story that is forced and dull. This method allows for greater flexibility in writing the play than would be the case if one wrote for specific puppet characters. In this case you need not worry about making creative puppets since puppets can be made imaginatively in so many ways.

Action and Dialogue

To have a play we must have a story to act, and dialogue to speak in a convincing and interesting manner. We must have characters that by their actions promote speech, which in turn promotes action throughout the play. It is difficult to say which comes first, speech or action, but if speech comes first it must give way to action, and vice versa. One promotes the other continually. It is not enough to have characters talking back and forth without any action. Action is very important for a good puppet play. Nor can you have a puppet narrate what has happened in a story or is about to happen and call it a puppet play.

The Introduction, the Body, the Conclusion

Just like any composition, a puppet play must have an introduction, a body, and a conclusion. For a dramatic puppet play, the introduction states a problem, the body develops a solution, and the conclusion solves the problem in a satisfying way. All the incidents of the play should move logically from the beginning, through the middle part to the end by means of action and dialogue.

Once we have a story to speak and act, the first thing in constructing a play is to have the character or characters faced with a problem immediately. It is best to present the problem in the beginning by action and not by mere statement of words. This action then leads to dialogue followed by more action, both necessary to the play in attempting to solve the problem. Thus by action and dialogue, the problem is satisfactorily solved in the end.

Characterization

In developing the plot, we must think of the characters in relation to the action. The personalities of the characters will influence the development of the plot by affecting what they say and do. Their characteristics will show in their speech and action. For example, in the play *Punch and Judy*, Punch is a clever rascal. He shows this consistently by what he says and does throughout the play.

Since the puppet stage is usually small, with room for only two puppeteers, it is wise not to have more than four puppet characters appear at one time for convenience— one on each hand of the puppeteers.

Therefore, in writing a puppet play, whether your own or based on a folk or fairy tale, it is important to keep in mind the number of characters which you will have. You can, of course, change puppets from time to time as needed and so have as many characters as you absolutely need in developing a play.

Adapting a Folk Tale to a Puppet Play

Folk tales are ideal for a puppet play. They have all the ingredients for a good action-filled performance. Usually there is a problem in the beginning, a middle part which attempts to solve the problem, and a proper ending which brings the problem to a satisfying conclusion. Besides, folk and fairy tales are full of wonderful fantasy, and puppets are perfect for fantasy. Being magical little people, they can do what we humans cannot.

Plots that have magical characters offer rich material to the puppeteer. For example, *Rumpelstiltskin* by the Brothers Grimm has all the excitement needed for a good puppet show. There is an immediate problem in the beginning when the miller, wishing to appear important in the eyes of the king, tells the king that he has a daughter who can spin gold out of straw. This information results in the miller's daughter going to the castle to spin gold out of straw for the king. Now we all know that she cannot do this. She has a problem. What happens? The supernatural enters the story. A little dwarf with magic powers appears who can do it for a token. Action takes place to resolve the problem. The dwarf spins gold out of straw for the miller's daughter.

However, the king's heart is greedy. He is not satisfied with one spinning, he must have more—more dialogue, which promotes more action. The little dwarf appears again and spins more gold for another token. This happens a third time. Now the miller's daughter has no more tokens to give. What is she to do? The dwarf asks her if she would give him her first child after she becomes queen. This she promises to do (more dialogue).

Does she keep her promise? Now the middle part of the story unfolds. Let us see what happens. After the miller's daughter becomes queen and her first child is born, the little dwarf returns to the castle (more action). He has come for what was promised him. But the queen begs him not to take away her child. She pleads so desperately that the little dwarf feels sorry for her. He tells her that she may keep the child if in three days she can guess his name. This dialogue gives way to more action.

The queen calls her messenger to her and tells him to go throughout the land searching for unusual and strange names (more dialogue). The dwarf appears twice, but each time the queen does not guess his name (more action and more dialogue).

Before the dwarf is to appear for the third time, the messenger returns on the third day (more action) with the information (more dialogue) that as he was returning home, just at the place where the fox meets the hare, he saw a strange sight. There was a queer little dwarf outside a cave, hopping on one leg around an open fire, and as he did this he sang:

"Today I bake; tomorrow I brew my beer;
The next day I will bring the queen's child here.
Ah! Lucky 'tis that no one doth know
Rumpelstiltskin is my name, ho, ho."

Here is dialogue that may solve the whole problem. Could the dwarf's name be "Rumpelstiltskin," thus saving the queen's child?

Now we come to the conclusion. When the little dwarf appears for the third and last time (more action) "Rumpelstiltskin" turns out to be the magic word (more dialogue). This causes the dwarf to kill himself in a rage (more action) and the queen keeps her child.

This folk tale contains all the ingredients for a dramatic puppet play. It is full of dialogue and action, each following the other naturally. It also involves superhuman power, which is ideal for puppetry.

To adapt *Rumpelstiltskin* to a puppet play we have to consider the following steps:

1. Immediately show what the problem is through dialogue. The miller tells the king that he has a daughter who can spin gold out of straw. The king, wishing to put her to the test, tells the miller to send his daughter to the castle.

2. Show what steps are taken, through action and dialogue, to solve the problem. This action and dialogue must follow in logical or natural order to bring the problem to a solution. A little dwarf appears who is instrumental in helping the miller's daughter solve her immediate problem. In so doing, he presents her with another problem. She must guess his name in three days. At first, the miller's daughter tries to do so unsuccessfully.

3. Show how the second problem is solved by means of a messenger. He brings the miller's daughter the magic word, "Rumpelstiltskin," which solves the whole problem.

In retelling an old tale, choose one that can be retold easily. Such stories as folk tales, fairy tales, myths, legends, Bible stories, and fables are excellent for adaptation. Select one that seems to you to be best suited to the particular type of puppet you wish to make and use. For example, select a story that has a great deal of dialogue for paper bag puppets since this type of puppet cannot be made to move very much. Also, it is important to choose a story you love and wish to share with others.

See what you can do with these tales: *The Emperor's New Clothes, The Swineherd, The Three Sillies, The Three Wishes, The Three Bears, The Three Little Pigs, Little Red Riding Hood, The Real Princess, Millions of Cats*, and many others. These folk tales have all the ingredients for an interesting and dramatic puppet play. They are short and easily adapted to a play. All you really need to do is make use of the dialogue, give the characters action, and you have a puppet play.

Writing an Original Puppet Play

Let us consider how to write an original puppet play, *A Visit From Outer Space,* which you will find in the back of the book on page 184. Using all the information that has been presented, the following are the steps to take:

1. Think about the kind of play you want. Will it be a fantasy, a mystery, science fiction, a humorous story, or a combination of these? Ours will be a science-fiction play.

2. Depending on the size of the stage to be used, consider the number of puppeteers and puppets you will have. This will determine how many characters to use at any one time. In our play we will have two puppeteers, each using two puppets at any one time.

3. Construct the plot or outline of the story, the incidents to be arranged in logical or natural order:

a. Two strange space travelers make an emergency landing with their space craft on Earth. This action takes place in the present time.

b. They do not like it on Earth and wish to return to their space world.

c. They cannot return because something is wrong with the engine of their space craft. This presents a problem. What will they do?

d. Space travelers look at their navigation chart to see exactly where they are. Luckily, they discover that they are close to an Earth space port.

e. They hike over to the space port.

f. Will they be able to hitch a ride back into space?

g. Just in time, they stow away in an Earth rocket ship which is about to take off.

h. Once inside, and the rocket ship is on its way, they make themselves known to the two astronauts.

i. Astronauts are not going to make a landing in outer space.

j. Space travelers cannot return to Earth with the astronauts since they cannot survive on Earth nor would they like to live there if they could. What will they do about it?

This chain of events has led us to a possible solution of the original problem.

k. The space travelers solve the whole problem by asking to be let off the rocket ship in which they are traveling when it is well into outer space. Being outer space creatures, they can float around in space until they are picked up by one of their own spaceships. This is done, solving the whole problem.

4. Following this outline, which develops in logical order, we have asked and answered the following questions:

a. Who? Space travelers.

b. What? Make an emergency landing.

c. Where? On Earth near a space port.

d. When? In the present time.

e. How? They return to outer space by hitching a ride aboard a space-bound rocket ship.

f. Why? Because they don't like it on Earth.

g. There are other questions answered in developing the story to a satisfying conclusion.

5. We have plunged into the problem immediately when the space travelers make a crash landing. This action shows, without a word being spoken, that here is a problem. The space travelers, through dialogue and action,

now show that they do not like it on Earth and wish to return to where they came from. However, they cannot do so since something is wrong with the engine of their spaceship. What will they do to solve this problem?

They consult their navigation chart and find that they are near a space port. Good! They will go there and try to hitch a ride back into space. This they do by stowing away on board a rocket ship which is about to take off. But the astronauts are not going to make a landing in space. How to solve the problem?

Since our travelers are outer space creatures, they can float in space until one of their own space craft picks them up. This becomes a satisfying solution to their problem.

6. Remember to have short, crisp dialogue. Long speeches become boring to the audience.

7. Action and speech should follow one another swiftly.

8. Characters in the play should be easily recognizable. Outer space creatures should really be out-of-this-world creatures by acting and talking like them. They don't like it here on Earth. This is a strange and dangerous place for them.

9. Consider in what order the characters will appear. This should be in logical order as the story develops.

10. In writing the play, always show the action that takes place by writing it in parenthesis after each character or in the dialogue as needed. Also show mood of speech in this manner (whispering, loud voice, anger, etc.).

11. The last step to consider is the type of puppet to use for the play. Here it would be best to use papier-mâché puppets since these can show greater action getting on and off the spaceship.

To summarize what is needed for adapting a folk and fairy tale, or an original story to a puppet play:

1. The story or plot must hold together by having a beginning with a problem, a middle which attempts to solve the problem, and a satisfying ending.

2. The story or plot must have plenty of action and dialogue, each following the other continuously in logical order.

3. The characters must remain constant with their characterization. If funny or worried, they must be so throughout the play.

4. The story should not take longer than 30 minutes to perform. This is long enough for an audience to sit through a show.

Ballads and Narrative Rhymes

Some puppet plays lend themselves very well to the use of a narrator, providing there is plenty of action in the story. For example, in the record of *Peter and the Wolf*, the narrator tells the whole story while the music sets the mood. The music and the narrator alternate while the puppets act out the story. I have used this particular record and technique very successfully with stick puppets as a shadow play. These stick or rod puppets can be used in front of the screen, like regular puppets, or behind the screen as shadows.

Narrated nursery rhymes and ballads can also be used in this manner. These rhymes and ballads are especially good for rod puppets in front of a backdrop or as shadow plays behind a screen.

See what you can do with some of the Mother Goose rhymes or the American ballads sung by Burl Ives.

{5} Stages

Puppet stages can be simple or complicated. However, for a beginner, I strongly recommend that you keep your stages as simple as possible. Here we shall deal only with simple, basic types of stages.

Fit the type of stage to the number of puppets appearing at one time. If your puppet play has several characters on stage at the same time, then it is necessary to have as large a space for movement as possible. You may even try performing without a stage.

No Stage

Experiment with no stage at all. It is possible to operate bag or hand puppets while you are in full view of the audience. Should you perform in this manner then it is a good idea to keep your own clothing as simple as possible. If your dress is too colorful or fancy there is the danger that you will distract the audience's attention from the puppets. However, if the puppets are interesting, and speak and act dramatically, the audience will focus their attention on them most of the time.

In my own school library, when I have had no time to prepare a puppet show with a stage setting or script, I have used this technique in telling a story with hand puppets. I have seen this type of performance done very effectively by professional Japanese puppeteers.

Try performing without a stage, using a puppet mask over your face. This can easily be made with a piece of construction paper onto which you draw facial features and cut holes for eyes, nose, and mouth. Then attach two pieces of string on either side to tie around your face. Move around with this mask as much as you like. We call this technique live puppetry. The ancient Greek actors performed in this manner. I have also seen this done interestingly by professional puppeteers.

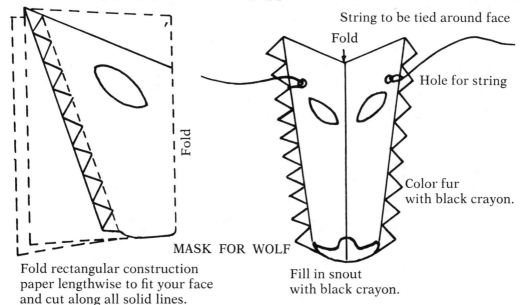

String to be tied around face

Fold

Hole for string

Color fur with black crayon.

Fold

MASK FOR WOLF

Fill in snout with black crayon.

Fold rectangular construction paper lengthwise to fit your face and cut along all solid lines.

Doorway Stage

This is an easy puppet stage to make. Just stretch a sheet across an open doorway to a height that is comfortable for you to perform in a kneeling position. Be sure your head is below the top of the sheet as you move the pup-

DOOR FRAME

Attach sheet with adhesive tape to door frame.

DOOR STAGE

pets. Fasten the sheet to the sides of the doorway with adhesive tape. You will be on one side of the stage while the audience sits on the other.

Windowsill Stage

A ground floor windowsill can also be used, with the puppeteers kneeling on the floor either inside the house or outside, while the audience is seated on the other side. Necessary props can be attached with Scotch or adhesive tape right on the sill without causing any damage. Of course it is difficult to use scenery with this type of stage.

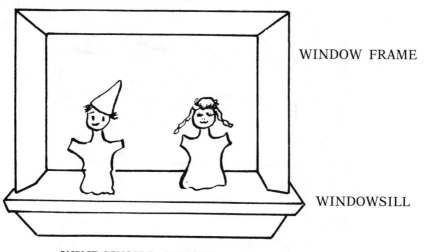

WINDOW FRAME

WINDOWSILL

WINDOWSILL STAGE

Table Stage

The top of a table is the simplest type puppet stage there is. With adhesive tape, attach an old sheet around the three sides of a table—left side, front and right side. Leave the back open where you will perform. Let the sheet hang down to the floor. This will hide you from your audience as you perform from the back, open side in a kneeling position. You can then use the top of the table as your stage to which you may attach props as needed. If the table is a large one, you can use many puppets at one time. However, the table stage makes it difficult to use scenery. If you must have scenery for effect, you can attach it to the wall behind the table with adhesive tape.

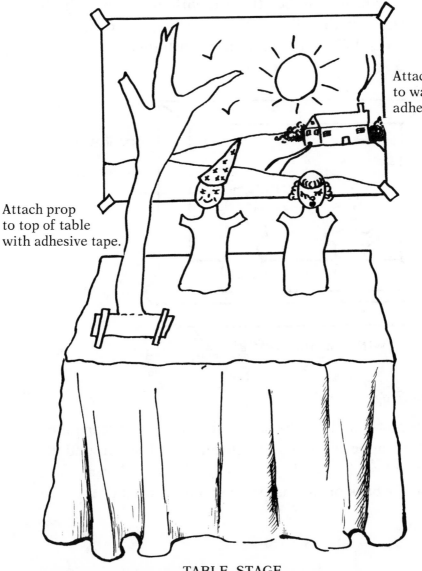

Attach scenery to wall with adhesive tape.

Attach prop to top of table with adhesive tape.

TABLE STAGE

Cardboard Box Stage

A cardboard box makes a nice, simple puppet stage. Attach a sheet to a table just as you did for the table stage. Use an empty oblong cardboard box which you can find in the food stores. Remove the top and bottom of the box. This will give you a cardboard frame with sides 1, 2, 3, 4. Set the box on one of its long sides onto the top of the table. Sit or kneel behind the open side of the table and let your puppets act within the box. It will depend on the size of the box as to how many puppets you can use at one time. A larger box will, of course, accommodate more puppets than a smaller one.

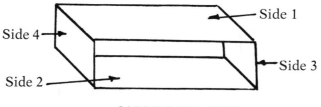

CARDBOARD BOX

Props can be used by attaching them with adhesive tape to the bottom of the box, which becomes the floor of the stage. Scenery, drawn or painted on construction or watercolor paper, can be used by attaching it to the top of the box along the back edge with adhesive tape and letting it hang down. This will act as a backdrop and will hide the top of your head or body when you kneel or sit behind the stage. You can then thrust your hands with your puppets under this backdrop onto the bottom of the cardboard stage. Use your imagination to decorate the cardboard box with either paints or crayons, or cover it with colorful paper.

Hang scenery down
from here with adhesive tape.

CARDBOARD BOX STAGE
Attach sheet to three sides of table, using adhesive tape.

Floor Length Stage

The professional type of puppet stage, which most puppeteers use, is the full length floor model. This is recom-
mended for the more advanced student of puppetry who
wishes to perform in as professional a manner as possible.

The floor length model shown in this chapter is similar to the one used by the children in my school library. It can be made with plywood or Masonite, which can be either cut by you or by the proprietor of the lumberyard where you obtain the material.

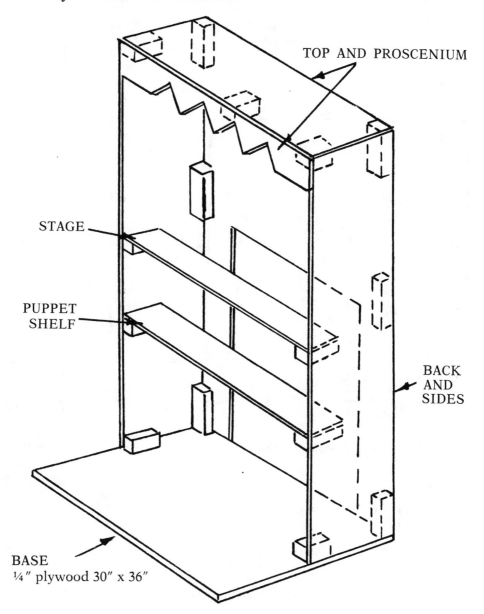

TOP AND PROSCENIUM

STAGE

PUPPET SHELF

BACK AND SIDES

BASE
¼" plywood 30" x 36"

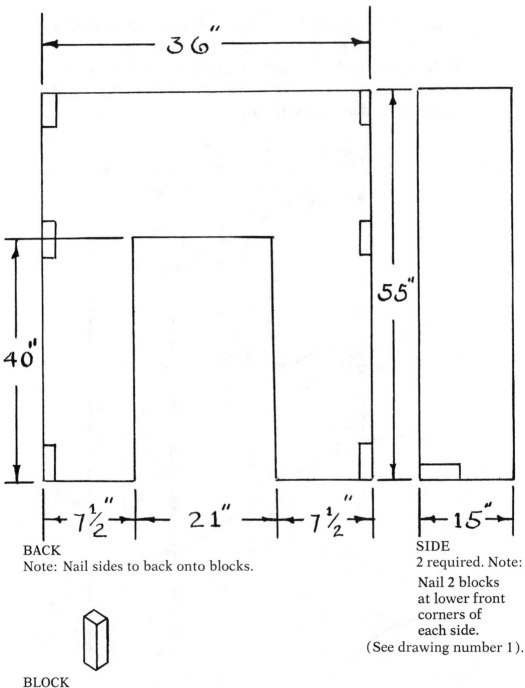

36"

55"

40"

7½"   21"   7½"   15"

BACK
Note: Nail sides to back onto blocks.

SIDE
2 required. Note:
Nail 2 blocks
at lower front
corners of
each side.
(See drawing number 1).

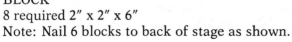

BLOCK
8 required 2" x 2" x 6"
Note: Nail 6 blocks to back of stage as shown.

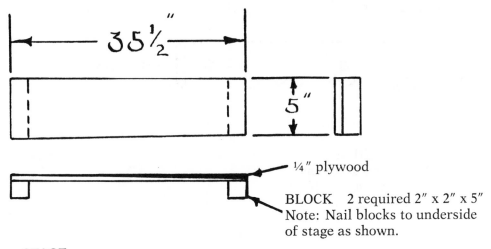

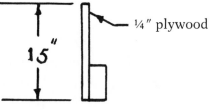

¼" plywood

BLOCK   2 required 2" x 2" x 5"
Note: Nail blocks to underside
of stage as shown.

STAGE

Note: Shelf beneath stage to be made exactly the same.
Place shelf 12 inches below stage (See drawing number 1).

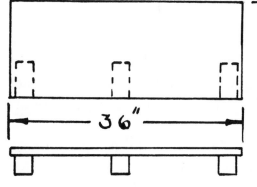

15"

¼" plywood

36"

Note: Nail 3 blocks—2" x 2" x 4"—
on underside of top as shown.
End blocks are to be
attached 5/16" in from sides.

TOP

137

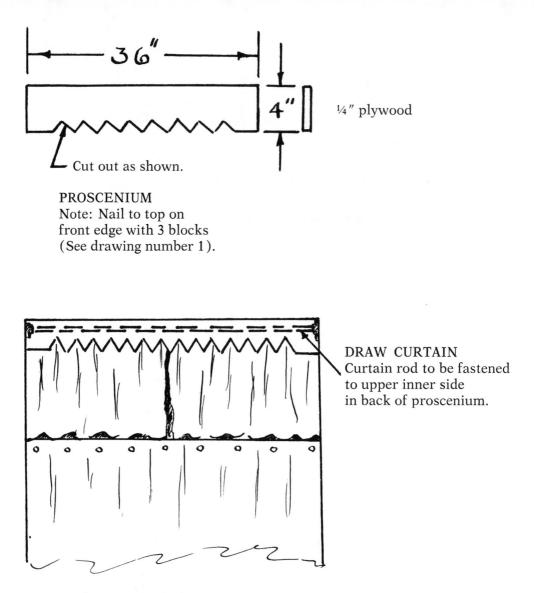

36"

4"

¼" plywood

Cut out as shown.

PROSCENIUM
Note: Nail to top on
front edge with 3 blocks
(See drawing number 1).

DRAW CURTAIN
Curtain rod to be fastened
to upper inner side
in back of proscenium.

This particular stage is designed to be used with a window shade for shadow puppets. Simply draw the shade down when needed and keep up when hand puppets are used.

To keep the stage simple, a curtain rod can be attached and the curtain drawn by hand when needed. Also, lights can be used as shown on the diagram or as described in the chapter, "Producing the Show."

SHADE
Shade brackets to be fastened to outer side of proscenium.

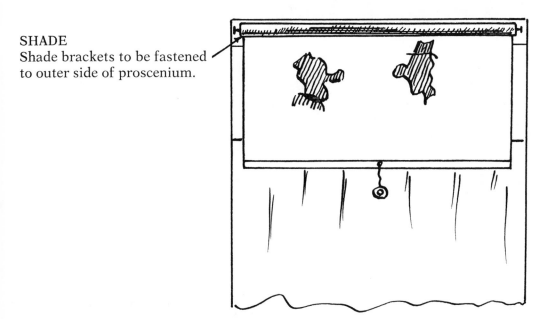

CURTAIN
Note: Curtain may be any solid-color material and tacked to front edge of stage.

Note: Attach scenery on inner back wall.

Two floodlights to be attached in upper corners and angled to light the stage.

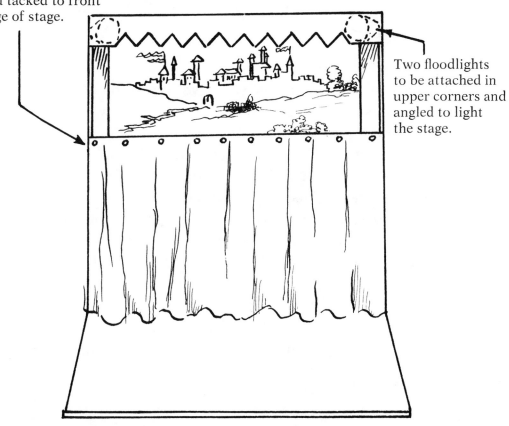

Producing the
{6} Show

Y ou have made the puppets, you have created the play, now let us consider how to produce a puppet show.

A puppet play is a story brought to life by means of movement and voice. The story is told through the puppets you manipulate, bringing them to life while you speak for them. This can be achieved by speaking slowly and deliberately, pausing now and then as though you are thinking about what you are saying. Even speaking hesitatingly as you would in real life is permissible.

Methods for Acting a Show

1. First there is the method of one puppeteer acting and speaking the show all by himself. This takes an experi-

enced person to do since he must carry out the entire show alone. He must change the puppets on his hands; change his voice from one puppet to another continually; attend to a possible change of scenery and even turn the pages of a script if he is using a script. All this is difficult to do alone and takes a great deal of practice.

A beginner puppeteer should not use this method. It is especially good, however, for an experienced puppeteer who does not use a script or props, but makes up a story as he goes along. Here there are no mechanical restrictions of props and scenery and the puppeteer can concentrate on the story itself.

2. The next method involves more than one puppeteer acting and speaking for each puppet. This is a simple method and especially good for the beginner. Where there are two puppeteers using four puppets (one on each hand) there can be a greater variety of voices, with the two performers changing for each puppet. Then, too, four hands can act out a play having more varied action and drama than two hands can. Two puppeteers can more easily change puppets and scenery, supply music, and attend to other necessary mechanics behind the stage than a single performer. However, it is advisable to have a stage-hand whenever possible to take care of these behind-the-stage duties.

3. A third method calls for one or more performers to move the puppets, while another supplies the voice for the puppet characters. This is rather difficult for a beginner since it is not easy to co-ordinate one's actions to another's voice. However, there is one type of performance where it can be used without difficulty. That is when puppets are used to act out the words of a narrator on a record. The recording of Prokofiev's *Peter and the Wolf,*

141

which I have given as a shadow play, lends itself very nicely to this method. Because the music alternates with the narration of the story, it gives the puppeteer time to act it out.

Such stories on records as *Rapunzel, The Real Princess, The Three Little Pigs,* and *Little Red Riding Hood* go with this method. Even though there is no music accompanying these stories, they are so well known that a puppeteer can manipulate the puppets and follow the story at the same time without difficulty.

This method is also good when singing or reading ballads and one does not have time to memorize a story. It is a method that lends itself to experimentation. Depending on how well the narrator and puppeteer co-operate, it can be very good or very bad.

Puppets in Action

1. Movement

Movement is the most important part of puppetry. Without it you cannot have a puppet show. Each type of puppet is made to move in different ways and each has its limitation of movement.

The bag puppet is moved by inserting your hand into the bag with four fingers resting at the bottom of the flap. By moving the fingers up and down against the palm of your hand, the flap opens and shuts.

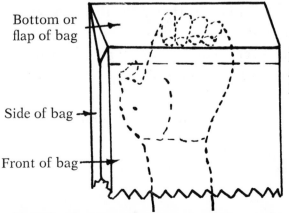

Bottom or flap of bag

Side of bag

Front of bag

Rest tips of fingers at edge of fold.
Move flap up and down.

The flat rod puppet simply has a support rod attached to the back which, held in your hand, moves back and forth.

The jointed rod puppet has two rods—a support rod and the control rod. The support rod holds the puppet upright. It is the control rod that moves only the joints by means of a wire or string system that can be attached to it.

The hand puppet is placed on your hand so that the index finger is in the hollow of the head and the thumb and third finger through the arm openings of the dress.

The limitation of movement will depend a great deal on the type of puppet being used.

The bag puppet can only open and shut its eyes or mouth.

Flat rod puppets can only be made to move back and forth.

Jointed rod puppets can move only at the joints and points of attachment to the control rod.

Hand puppets have a greater range of movement. They can move almost as well as humans do. They can be made to jump up and down, walk, clap hands, wave arms, turn the head, bend, and pick up objects.

For a hand puppet to clap hands, simply bring together the thumb and third finger repeatedly. To wave, move one finger up and down. To walk, twist your wrist in even movements to imitate a right and left movement of imaginary legs. Raising the wrist takes the puppet off the floor and lowering it puts it back on the floor. To make a bow, bend your wrist and at the same time slightly bend the index finger in the head. Thumb and third finger, which are the puppet's arms, should be bent in a graceful way.

Usually a puppet's lips do not move. However, you can help your audience know that a puppet is talking by having it move ever so slightly as it is speaking, while the other puppets on stage remain motionless until it is their turn to speak.

Puppets are limited not only to movement but also to facial expression. If a puppet is to cry at one time and laugh the next time, it can do only one or the other while it is on your hand. It is difficult to work with two puppets of the same character, one showing laughter and the other weeping. Therefore, in constructing such a puppet try to keep this in mind and fashion the facial features midway between the two extremes of laughter and weeping.

Remember, puppet actions should be definite and deliberate to the point of exaggeration if necessary. They are little people and their actions must be seen by an audience. Move your arm and puppet slowly and deliberately, not fast and jerkily. Actions should be clear, simple, and smooth. Don't knock your puppets around the stage to show action. Feel the movements as though you were moving your own body, through your arm and into the puppet you are holding.

Know your puppet characters as you would real people. Try to understand why they act as they do. Practice and experiment with different movements to achieve different effects.

2. Voice and Personality

Speak clearly, distinctly, enunciating each word, and with volume even if you are speaking for a little person.

This does not mean that you have to shout to be heard. On the contrary. Just be sure you are projecting your voice so that the people in the last row of the audience can hear you. If a puppet stage is being used, remember that it stands between you and the audience, and therefore it has a tendency to muffle the sound of your voice.

If possible, speak with the help of a microphone. One that is attached around your neck is best. If you use a floor-type model, be sure to set it at the same level with your lips so that you speak right into it. While you sit, kneel, or stand before it, test it for clarity before starting your show.

It is best for each puppeteer to speak for the puppet he is manipulating. If you are speaking for two different puppets, try to change your voice so the audience can distinguish one from the other. This can be done by pitching your voice at a higher or lower level consistently for each. Keep these voices the same throughout so that the audience knows who is speaking.

It is best for a boy to take a boy's part and a girl to take a girl's part. Also, your voice should try to fit the characteristics of the puppets—fearful, gay, mischievous, bragging, and so on. A man's voice should be deep; a small child's voice will be high-pitched; an old person's voice will be shaky; a frightened voice will sound hesitant; a witch's voice will be shaky and high-pitched at the same time.

Whenever possible, speak in your own natural voice unless you are taking the part of a special character. If you are taking the part of a special character, let your puppet speak according to the personality he is supposed to be. If he is an excited person let him speak fast and excitedly. If he is a lazy person, speak slowly as if you want to go to sleep.

In our Punch-and-Judy play, Punch is a braggart who speaks in a loud, boisterous voice, slightly squeaky and high-pitched. Judy is very much disgusted and annoyed with Punch and so her voice must show this. The baby's voice should be squeaky and high-pitched. The policeman has a deep voice and should speak with authority. The doctor should also speak with authority. Scaramouch, being an artist, should speak in gay, careless tones. The hangman, a serious character, should speak in low tones and at a slow rate. The devil, a mysterious fellow, should have a deep, commanding voice. And, of course, the dog Toby should bark with anger at Punch.

Let your voice come from the very bottom of your chest. Try to do all this without screaming, shouting, or straining, or your voice will become so tired you will be hoarse.

Remember that the personality of the puppet, which is a very important part of the show, comes through by means of his voice as well as action. Experiment and practice. It is fun to try different voices.

Placement of the Stage

A stage must be in full view of the audience. Therefore, place it in the front and center of the audience. Do not ever place it in front of windows since the light from the windows will interfere with seeing the puppets clearly. A light from behind an object will have a tendency to place that object in darkness, creating almost a silhouette effect. Also, it is very hard on the eyes of the audience to keep staring into a bright light. If you must place the stage in front of a window, pull the shade down and be sure to use spotlights on the puppets.

Scenery

A puppet show will be more effective with as little scenery as possible. With fewer interruptions which are necessary for changing scenes, the audience's attention will be focused on the puppets rather than distracted by elaborate and frequent change of scenery. It is better to keep the story flowing continually than to stop to change a scene and break its spell.

It is possible to have a puppet show with no scenery. The Punch-and-Judy show requires no scenery at all. Since a great deal of the play depends upon the clever exchange of words, it can be performed before drawn curtains throughout without scenery. The audience is concerned only with the speech and action of the puppets.

It is also possible to have only one scene if the greater part of the story takes place in one place as in *Rumpelstiltskin*. Include in your scenery only that which is part of the story to lend atmosphere and mood. In *Rumpelstiltskin* you can have a scene showing the interior of the king's castle where the miller's daughter is to spin gold out of straw. It could show a window since, in the story, the little dwarf appears through the window even though you do not actually use it for his entrances and exits. You can simply make him appear from underneath the puppet stage and disappear the same way. The beginning of the story could take place before a drawn curtain.

For atmosphere, you may like to include in your scenery a very fancy chandelier with candles. Remember, this

147

is the interior of the king's castle and as such it is most likely to be fashionable and rich looking.

You should not only include in your scene whatever is part of the story, but be sure that the objects fit into the time of the story. In other words, do not draw a modern-looking window or chandelier for a story which takes place a long time ago.

To show three different rooms with the same scenery, when the "king showed her to a larger room filled with lots more straw" you can simply close the curtain, change the position of the spinning wheel to a different part of the stage, and reopen the curtain using the same scene.

Scenery can be drawn directly on a white construction board with black or colored crayons. It can also be two-dimensional, where pieces of scenery are drawn on colored paper or colored with crayon on white paper. These pieces can then be cut and pasted on a background of heavy construction paper large enough to fit the backdrop of the stage.

Keep your scenery as simple as possible. Do not crowd it with too many objects since this may become distracting to the audience. Use construction paper or cardboard large enough to cover the backdrop of the stage. Draw with colored crayons or paint with watercolor or even use a dark drawing pencil if that is all you have.

When the scenery is completed to your satisfaction, simply attach it to the backdrop of the stage with thumbtacks or Scotch Tape.

Above all, remember to keep your scenes simple and few in number. The less scenery, the greater the continuity of the story and concentration on the puppets.

Properties

Properties, or props, are three-dimensional objects such as missiles, automobiles, spinning wheels, chairs, straw, yarn, trees, and so on which are used by the puppets to develop the story. They are more important than scenery. However, use only what is necessary to develop the story and keep them simple.

In the story *Rumpelstiltskin,* it is absolutely necessary to have a small spinning wheel. If you also wish to have a chair for the little dwarf to sit on, do so if you can manage it without too much trouble. Otherwise eliminate it, for your puppet can appear behind the spinning wheel in a sitting position by merely bending your wrist slightly. Straw and yellow yarn for gold are also necessary to have for props since your story involves these materials. If your stage is large enough and not overcrowded, you may, if you like, construct a window. However, it is not really necessary.

For *Peter and the Wolf* it is essential to have a tree and a slip-knot lasso for Peter, who sits in the tree to lasso the wolf.

Props may be constructed with heavy construction paper, either white or colored, and also with cardboard, plywood, and Masonite. In addition, you will need a ruler, scissors, pencil, glue, and possibly a hammer and nails. Of course Scotch or adhesive tape for securing the props to the stage will also be helpful. Materials that may be fashioned into props used by the puppets include pipe-cleaners for eyeglasses, cotton for beards and moustache, a wooden stick for a wand or shaped into a gun and attached to the hand of a puppet.

Be sure that the size of your props is in correct proportion to your puppets. In other words, you cannot have a large puppet and a tiny chair or a large puppet and a tiny tree. They should be just the right size for each other.

When not in use, properties can be kept on the table or shelf behind the puppet stage with the puppets.

Again, let me caution you, the fewer props the better. It has been my experience that the more properties used, the greater is the chance of knocking them down during a performance. Remember, the stage is usually small and puppets do have to move around, and in so doing can easily knock down the props.

Lighting

Lighting can be as simple or as elaborate as you wish it to be. Of course, for a beginner, it is wise to keep the mechanics of lighting as simple as possible. Here we shall deal only with simple lighting.

Your puppets, scenery, props, and play are all wasted, no matter how good they are, if they cannot be clearly seen by the audience.

The simplest lighting to use is an ordinary goose-neck desk lamp. It can be set on the floor, either to the right or left, about one third in from the side of the puppet stage. The lamp can be moved at any angle that will best show the puppets without casting too many shadows. Try using two of these, one on each side of the stage for better effect. They can also be clamped on to the front of the stage to throw light on the puppets.

A spotlight is another kind of light to use on the floor. Be sure that it is tilted upward to throw light on the puppets so that they can be clearly seen from the back of the room. Experiment with the placement of the spotlight so that there will be a minimum of shadow cast on the puppets. Sometimes, placing a spotlight directly in front of a puppet with strong accented features will cause these features to fade away and become flat.

Two spotlights can also be installed inside the stage in the upper right- and left-hand corners, as shown in the diagram for the floor stage.

A 35-millimeter slide projector can also be used if available. This has to be placed on a stand or table to the side of the puppet stage. Experiment with the right position as you did for the lamps.

Remember to place these lights where they will not be touched, since they become very hot.

Using the Script

There is more than one way of using the script of a puppet play. Choose the technique best suited for you.

1. The ideal puppet play should be given without reading the script or memorizing it word for word. This is the way the early professional puppeteers put on their puppet shows to keep the presentation natural, spontaneous, and fresh. This created a feeling among the audience that the play was actually being made up at that moment.

Read the script aloud beforehand over and over again, letting it soak in your mind. Pay particular attention to dramatic words and phrases which add to the interest of the play. See the events in your mind's eye, letting them form a series of moving pictures. Know the sequence of these moving mental pictures so well that you can reproduce them with words making no reference to the script.

151

When you are able to do this smoothly and with confidence, you can then put on a puppet show without referring to a script in front of you. If it makes you feel more secure to have it spread out before you while performing, then by all means do so. However, try not to depend on the script once you have learned it. This will enable you to concentrate on manipulating the puppets, which you can easily forget to do while reading from a script.

2. Another way of using the script is to have it before you, reading it dramatically while performing. It is my experience that a puppet play can be read as though you were talking naturally, provided you know the script beforehand well enough. If you do read the script, do not concentrate so much on the words that you forget to act the puppets. Remember that speech must move the puppets.

Here again, before putting on a performance, read the play aloud several times, paying particular attention to dramatic words and phrases. Underscore them in red to alert yourself when reading the script during a performance. If you can put on a dramatic reading with sincerity and enthusiasm, it will result in an audience's feeling that the performance is being made up at the moment.

Placement of Script

A sensitive microphone, if you use one, as suggested earlier, will easily pick up the sound of a person turning the pages of a script. Therefore, Scotch Tape or glue each page of the script onto a piece of cardboard and place them side by side on the shelf behind the stage where the puppeteer sits. If the script is long, it can be attached to both sides of the cardboard in such a manner that all you need to do is to turn them over from left to right in consecutive order for the continuation of the play. For example, suppose your script consists of eight pages, paste pages 1 to 4 on each cardboard and pages 5 to 8 on the reverse of each. When you finish performing the script of page 4, either you, if you have only one puppet on your hand, your partner puppeteer, or the stagehand, can turn over the first cardboard to page 5 and so on to page 8.

Placement of Puppets

Puppets that are not on your hand but are to be used later on in the play can easily be kept either on a shelf behind the stage if you have shelf space, or on your lap. Each puppeteer must keep on his lap only the puppets which he will be working with. Also, if two puppeteers are working together, it would be wise for each to take the role of one puppet which appears for a good part of the play and one which does not. This would cut down the number of times a puppeteer has to change puppets.

For example, in *Rumpelstiltskin* one puppeteer can have on one hand the miller's daughter, who appears a good part of the time and on the other, the king, who does not. The second puppeteer can have on one hand the little dwarf, who also appears frequently, and on the other hand the messenger, who does not. Naturally the one hand which does not hold a puppet too long will be the hand to change to another small-part character.

It is best to have another person behind the stage as a stagehand who assists with the work of changing puppets or even to take the part of a character if necessary.

153

Using Music

For a beginner, music is best used before a puppet show starts to set a mood or atmosphere. For example, if possible, use a record of carnival music before introducing Punch and Judy while the audience is assembling in their seats. Music can also be used during scenery changes that are rather long; during intermission time for a long performance; or at the end of a show.

Do not attempt to use music during a performance until you are a more experienced puppeteer. If you do use music this way, be sure that you make a suitable choice. Play the record through and mark off on the script where you will want it lowered or stopped. Rehearse it through with your puppets to see if the actions of the puppets will fit in with the type of music. Have a stagehand help you to attend to the mechanics of lowering or stopping the record while you are performing. Music is most challenging and effective as a background for a Valentine or circus story. If a puppet story is based on the use of music, such as in *Peter and the Wolf* and ballads, then by all means use it.

In a performance with music, place the record player on a table behind the puppet stage out of the audience's view so as not to break the spell of action and music.

Experiment with music as you grow more confident in your ability as a puppeteer. It lends itself to wonderful possibilities for a more creative and interesting puppet show.

Rehearsals

Keep rehearsals to a minimum. A puppet show that is

rehearsed over and over again will lose its spontaneity if *every* word and action is memorized beforehand.

If performing alone, try to remember the order of appearance of the puppets. Keep your words and actions as spontaneous as possible even if you are reading from a script.

When performing with other puppeteers, it is essential for each to know the part the other is to speak and act. It is absolutely necessary that each knows the "cue words" of the other at all times. These are the last words of each puppeteer's performance. Then each puppeteer will know when to start his own lines.

Placement of Chairs for Audience

Start the first row from five to seven feet from the stage. Place the chairs in a semicircle before the stage, so that each row will have a chair between the two chairs in front of it. This will eliminate the need for a person stretching his neck to see between the two heads in front of him. Do not swing the end chairs out too far since these viewers will have difficulty seeing the puppets.

Things to Remember in Producing a Puppet Show

If there is to be more than one puppeteer, work out a backstage position for each according to the position you will want the puppets to appear on stage before the audience. Remember that your right-hand puppet will appear to the left of the audience and the left-hand puppet to the right.

Be aware of keeping your puppet erect on the stage. There is a tendency for your hand to become tired and to droop while manipulating the hand puppet. This will cause your puppet to slouch over and the audience will not see its face clearly. The best thing to do is rest the front part of your wrist on the stage, which will give you support and help keep the puppet erect. Rod puppets should be held by the rod so that the whole body part appears to rest on the stage. Simple bag puppets are easy to hold. Merely keep your hand high enough on the stage so that the whole puppet is viewed by the audience.

The puppet's height should be constant, not tall at one time and short the next. Remember, when a child or small puppet is shown, to hold your hand lower.

The puppets should be facing one another while talking to each other rather than looking out at the audience. When they do not talk to each other they may face the audience.

Have as many theater helpers as needed and be sure that each knows his duties before a performance. The ushers have charge of the seating of the audience. They must be sure that the smallest children sit up front, that the doors are closed and the window blinds are drawn. They inform the stagehand when the audience is ready for the show to begin.

The stagehand then takes over and attends to operating the spotlights or film projector. He is also in charge of the record player if music is used, either while the audience is assembling, during intermission, or at the end of the show when the audience is leaving.

Puppet Plays

{7}

Rumpelstiltskin

Characters:	*Properties:*
Miller	Spinning Wheel
King	Chair
Miller's Daughter	Straw
Dwarf	Yellow Yarn
Messenger	Necklace
	Ring
	A small bundle for the Queen's baby

Setting:

Before a drawn curtain, miller appears with his daughter, then the king. The king looks at the miller's daughter and turns around. He is about to leave when the miller detains him.

Act I

Miller (bowing low): Good morning, your Majesty. Good morning. May I present my beautiful daughter? You may not believe it, but she can spin gold out of straw.

King (turns again, incredulous): Gold out of straw? No, I don't believe it. But we'll soon find out if what you say is true. I command you to send your daughter to my castle tomorrow morning and I'll put her to the test. (Exits)

Mistress Miller (very disturbed, almost frantic): But father, you *know* I can't spin gold out of straw. How can I possibly go to the castle?

Miller (apologetically): I was only trying to appear important in the eyes of the king.

Mistress Miller (frightened): What shall I do now?

Miller: My dear, the king has commanded you to go to the castle. You have no choice now but to go.

Mistress Miller (crying): Oh dear! Oh dear! What will happen to me? What will happen to me? (Curtain closes.)

Act II
At the King's Castle

When the curtain rises there is a spinning wheel in a corner, a chair and a small pile of straw on the floor. Hidden below stage is another small pile of yellow yarn.

King: Well, Mistress Miller, I see you have come to spin

all this straw into gold. Now sit yourself down and spin gold for me. If by tomorrow morning you have not done so, you shall die. (Exits)

Mistress Miller (crying with her head in her hands): Oh dear me, I can't spin gold out of straw! What shall I do? What shall I do?

Dwarf (appears suddenly from under stage or through a window): Well, well, Mistress Miller. And why are you crying so?

Mistress Miller (lifting her head up): Ah me! Why shouldn't I cry? I have to spin gold out of this straw, and don't know how to do it.

Dwarf: What will you give me if I do it for you?

Mistress Miller: My necklace. (Takes necklace off and gives it to the dwarf.)

Dwarf (takes the necklace and puts it around his neck. He then sits down before the spinning wheel, takes straw from the floor, transfers it to spinning wheel, and makes it disappear below stage. Then he picks up yellow yarn from below stage and pretends to spin it out): Whee—whee—whee! Look at it turning to gold! (He does this until all the straw has disappeared below stage and the yellow yarn is piled up by his side.) There, now, Mistress Miller, you have nothing to worry about. All the straw has been spun into gold. Good luck to you! (Disappears below stage.)

Mistress Miller (delighted): Thank you, thank you, little man.

King (appears and is astonished): My goodness! You *can* spin gold out of straw! My boots and saddle! I can hardly believe it! Now let's see what you can do this time. Come with me. (Curtain closes. When it reopens, the spinning wheel is in another part of the

159

stage, to show another room, with lots more straw than before. King and Mistress Miller enter.) Do you see this straw?

Mistress Miller: Yes, your Majesty.

King: Let me see what you can do this time, Mistress Miller. Sit yourself down and spin this straw into gold; and if you have not done so by tomorrow morning, you shall lose your life. (Exits)

Mistress Miller (again cries despairingly, with her head in her hands): Oh, me! What shall I do? What shall I do?

Dwarf (enters again): Well, well, in trouble again. What will you give me if I spin it once more?

Mistress Miller (relieved): Oh! Little man. I will give you the ring off my finger. (Takes ring off and hands it to dwarf who takes it and puts it on his finger.)

Dwarf (sits himself down before the spinning wheel and again makes the straw gradually disappear below stage while picking up and measuring out arm lengths of yellow yarn into a pile as before): Wheee—wheee—wheee! Look at it turning to gold! (This goes on till all straw disappears.) Now you need not cry any more, Mistress Miller. Good luck! (Disappears)

Mistress Miller (again appreciatively): Thank you! Thank you! Thank you! (Fingers the yellow yarn.)

King (appears, more surprised than before): My saddle and boots! You did it again! How marvelous! How wonderful! I'll tell you what I'll do. Spin it just once more. Come with me. (Curtain closes and when it reopens the spinning wheel has again been moved to a different position and there is lots more straw than before. King and Mistress Miller enter.) Now, sit yourself down and once more spin all this straw into gold. If you do, I shall make you my queen. If not, you will forfeit your life. (Exits)

Mistress Miller (crying): Oh, me! Oh, me! What shall I do now? What shall I do?

Dwarf (appears again): Again? What will you give me this time if I spin gold for you?

Mistress Miller (very sad): Alas! I have nothing more to give you.

Dwarf: Will you promise to give me your first child after you become queen?

Mistress Miller: Yes, yes, I promise!

Dwarf (sits down before spinning wheel and again spins gold by making straw disappear below stage and heaps yellow yarn in a pile): There now, it's all done. Remember your promise! (Exits)

Mistress Miller (happily): Oh, thank you, thank you! Yes, I'll remember.

King (appears while Mistress Miller is fingering the gold): Well, well, well! I see you've done it again. I could not ask for a richer wife. Come, you shall become my queen. (King takes Mistress Miller by the hand and both exit. Draw curtain.)

Act III

In the Queen's Room

Queen (cradles her baby in her arms and hums a lullaby): How happy I am. I not only am queen, but also mother to a beautiful child. My pretty little girl. (Suddenly she looks up.)

Dwarf (appears suddenly before the queen with a gleeful

voice): Ah! Now, my queen, I have come for what you promised me a year ago!

Queen (tightens her hold on her child): Oh, no! No, I cannot give her to you. I'll give you all my jewels and you can become very rich.

Dwarf: I have no need for jewels. I would rather have something living than all the treasures in the world!

Queen (cries frantically): Oh, please, please, don't take her from me! I beg you, I beg you not to!

Dwarf (feels sorry for the queen): Well—I will give you three days in which to guess my name. If within that time you do, you shall keep your child. (Exits) (Curtain draws with queen crying.)

Queen (curtain reopens with queen alone): Ah, me, I couldn't sleep all night thinking of all the names I have ever heard. I even sent my messenger all over the country to inquire what other names there are. I hope I have the right name for the dwarf.

Dwarf (appears suddenly): And now, your Majesty, what's my name?

Queen: Is it Casper?

Dwarf: No! That's not my name!

Queen: Is it Melchior?

Dwarf: Nope! That's not my name!

Queen: Is it Balzer?

Dwarf: Nope! Not my name, not my name, not my name!

Queen: I'll try again tomorrow.

Dwarf (gleefully): You'll never guess my name! Never guess my name! (Exits, jumping up and down. Curtain is drawn for a while, then reopens.)

Queen (very sleepy): I'm so tired. I was awake all night again thinking and inquiring of unusual and strange names. Oh, I do hope I can guess the dwarf's name.

Dwarf (appears suddenly and teasingly): Have you guessed my name? Have you?

Queen (hopefully): Is it—Cowribs?

Dwarf: Nope! Not my name!

Queen: Is it—Spindleshanks?

Dwarf: Nope! Not my name!

Queen: Is it—Fancy Pants?

Dwarf (hopping around gleefully): Nope! Not my name, not my name, not my name! Never mind. You have one more day. Good luck for tomorrow! (Exits, hopping and shouting.) Not my name, not my name, not my name! (Curtain closes with queen sobbing, with her head in her hands. After a while curtain reopens.)

Queen (very sadly): Here it is the third and last day. If I don't guess the dwarf's name today, I will lose my child. Oh, dear, what shall I do, what shall I do?

Messenger (enters and bows low): My queen.

Queen (hopefully): My good messenger. Have you found any new names? Have you?

Messenger: No, I haven't. But on my way home, as I turned the corner of a mountain, I saw a strange sight. In front of a cave at the foot of the mountain, there was a fire burning in the open. Around the fire, I saw a strange little man hopping first on one foot and then on the other. And as he hopped, he sang:

Today I bake; tomorrow I brew my beer;
The next day I will bring the queen's child here.
Ah! Lucky 'tis that no one doth know
Rumpelstiltskin is my name, ho! ho!

Queen (delighted): Oh! My good messenger. If that is the right name, I shall reward you well. You may go now. (Messenger exits.)

Queen (hopefully): Could it be Rumpelstiltskin?

Dwarf (appears suddenly): Now, your Majesty, what's my name?

Queen (pretending to be anxious): Could it be—Kunz?

Dwarf: No! That's not my name!

Queen: Is it—Heinz?

Dwarf: Nope. Not my name!

Queen: Is it by chance—Rumpelstiltskin?

Dwarf (shrieking): Arrrrrr! The devil told you that, the devil told you that! (He stamps and shrieks till he falls down below the stage.)

Queen: Now I can live happily with my husband and child! (She bows to audience. Curtain closes.)

Punch and Judy

Note: Punch-and-Judy shows are very much alike wherever you see them. Although there may be a slight difference in each, due to each puppeteer improvising, they are very much like the one presented here. Use this basic play to start with, but to have your very own Punch-and-Judy show, try to interject any additional character and humorous saying you may invent.

Characters:

Punch	Scaramouch
Judy	Policeman
Baby	Hangman
Toby	Devil

Properties:

Sticks

Gallows with a slip-knot rope attached

Punch, with his high cheekbones, curved long nose pointing down to his bony upturned chin, sports a tricornered hat.

At Curtain Rise:

The whole play is performed before a drawn curtain. Punch peeps out first from one side of curtain then from the other, then from the middle, waving his hand at the audience each time. He comes out from behind the curtain and starts counting the audience—pointing with his finger.

Punch: One—Two—Three—Four—Five—Oh, boy! Watch
    and see! Just see and watch!
    Ladies and Gentlemen
    Pray how do you do?
    If I make you happy
    I am happy too.
    Come and hear my merry little play,
    If I do not make you laugh,
    I need not make you pay.

Punch (claps his hands and dances while singing):
    For he's a jolly good fellow
    For he's a jolly good fellow
    For he's a jolly good fe-el-low!
    Which nobody can deny!
    Judy! Oh Judy! Come, my proud beauty!

Toby (dog enters instead): Bow! Wow! Wow!

Punch: Oh, hello, Toby! Who called you? How do you do,
    Mr. Toby? Hope you're very well, Mr. Toby!

Toby: Bow! Wow! Wow!

Punch (approaching very cautiously): I'm glad to hear
    it, Toby! What a nice, good dog you are! Good Toby,
    nice Toby!

Toby (growls): Arrr-rrr! Arrr-rrr!

Punch (attempts to pat Toby on the head): Good doggie!
    Good doggie! Be a good doggie and I'll give you a
    pail of water and a broomstick for supper!

Toby the dog has a sharp, pointed nose and an opened mouth showing his sharp teeth.

Toby (snaps at Punch's hand): Arrr-rrr! Arrr-rrr!

Punch (strikes Toby with stick which he has tied to his hand): Toby! You're one bad dog! Here take this, and this, and this! Get away with you!

Toby (bites Punch's nose): Arrr-rrr! Arrr-rrr! Arrr-rrr!

Punch (holds his nose with one hand and cries): Oh, my nose, my nose, my poor nose! My poor, poor nose! (Strikes Toby with stick.) Here take this, and this, and this, you beast!

Toby (runs off stage crying): Awrr-rr! Awrr-rr! Awrr-rr!

Punch (holding his nose): There, I showed him who's boss. Oh, my nose! My poor, poor nose! Help! Police! Doctor! Help, my nose!

Doctor (enters slowly with stick tied to his hand): Yes, yes, Mr. Punch, what is the matter? Where does it hurt?

Punch (still holding his nose): My nose, kind old doctor, my pretty little nose!

Doctor (approaches Punch, then looks at Punch's toes): Your pretty little toes. Yes, yes.

Punch: Look closer, kind old doctor. My toes are fine. (Kicks doctor.) See???

Doctor: Ah-ha! You have a bad case, Mr. Punch, but I have just the medicine for you. (Hits Punch with his stick.) Come and take your medicine, Mr. Punch! Whack! Whack!

Punch: Oh, no more medicine, good kind doctor. I feel better already. I must pay your bill now. (Hits doctor with stick.) Here take this, and this, and this! (Punch hits the doctor so hard, the doctor falls down dead.) Ah-ha-ha! You took your pay very well! (Picks up doctor and throws him over stage.) Out you go! And

The Doctor, a learned man, has a long beard and wears a white smock.

good riddance to you! (Punch sings and dances around stage.)

For he's a jolly good fellow

For he's a jolly good fellow

For he's a jolly good fe-el-low

Which nobody can deny.

Scaramouch (enters and stands glaring at Punch.)

Punch (stops dancing and singing): I say, old man, who are you?

Scaramouch: I'm not an old man. But what do *you* say?

Punch: I say, I say, old horse?

Scaramouch: Old horse? I'm not an old horse! But what do you say?

Punch: I say!

Scaramouch: I know. You've said it three times already. What do you have to say for yourself?

Punch: I've got a lot to say, only I don't like to brag.

Scaramouch: Oh, you don't like to brag? Then don't.

Punch: You see, I can't talk without bragging because the truth about me sounds like bragging. Look at me, I can't help it if I am handsome, can I? And my beautiful nose! The biggest and the best in this town. (Sings)

Nose, nose, jolly red nose!

Guess what gave me this jolly red nose!

Scaramouch: What, Mr. Punch?

Punch: I'll tell you. Eating red apples. That's what. And look at my eyes! See them twinkle? And I'm rich! And I'm strong as a lion! I can lick anybody here! (Looks at audience.) Who wants to try out there? Anybody?

Scaramouch: Come on and lick me.

Scaramouch, a musician, with a long moustache and pointed beard, wears a beret.

Punch: No, not in my Sunday clothes. You expect a gentleman to fight in his best Sunday clothes? Wait until I get on my overalls. I tell you, I was a great beau in my day. See all those pretty girls out there? (Points to audience.) Well, they came to see me. (Sings and dances.) Mother, Mother, I want to marry Pretty Punch, Puncinello!

But girls, I'm already married. Didn't you know I was married? My wife—she is named Judy. That means, beauty. Judy—Beauty. (Turns to Scaramouch.) You know Judy, don't you? She's a grand old girl. But she fights, so I have to knock her down. You ought to hear her holler when I do!

Scaramouch: Well, Mr. Punch! You call yourself a gentleman and you hit a lady???

Punch: I *am* a gentleman. But I have a quick temper. I love my Judy. She is so beautiful. She has a nose just like mine. But she's not as beautiful as *I* am!

Scaramouch: Mr. Punch, you are a braggart!

Punch: No, I'm not!

Scaramouch: Yes, you are!

Punch (points his stick, which is tied to his hand, at Scaramouch, takes aim and then marches right up to him and whacks him on his head): No, I'm not, I tell you! Whack! Whack! Whack!

Scaramouch: Ow-www! Ow-www! Ow-www! (Holds his head with his hand.) I shall make you pay for my head, Sir!

Punch: And I shall make you pay for my stick, Sir!

Scaramouch: I haven't broken your stick.

Punch: And I haven't broken your head!

Scaramouch (still holding his head): You have, Sir!

Punch: Then it must have been cracked before!

Scaramouch: Besides, you struck my dog, Toby.

Punch: He isn't your dog!

Scaramouch: He *is* my dog!

Punch: No, he isn't.

Scaramouch: He *is*, I tell you! Last night I lost him.

Punch: And last night I found him!

Scaramouch: We'll soon see whether he belongs to you. We'll fight for him. Now, don't begin till I say "Time." (Punch knocks Scaramouch down with his stick.) Ow-www! That wasn't fair!

Punch: It *was* fair! I didn't hit you till you said "Time."

Scaramouch: I never did! I only said, Don't begin till I say, "Time."

Punch (knocks Scaramouch down again with his stick): There, you said it again!

Scaramouch: Here, Toby, here, Toby! Come help your master.

Punch: No, no, don't call him! It isn't fair! You didn't say "Time." Oh dear! Oh dear! (Holds his nose with his hand.) My nose! My poor nose! My pretty little nose! Please, please don't call him!

Scaramouch: You are a coward, Sir! A coward, indeed!

Punch (aims his stick at Scaramouch, then marches toward him still pointing his stick): I'll show you who's a coward! (Whacks Scaramouch's head till he falls down dead.) There, that will teach him! (Kicks Scaramouch off the stage. Sings and dances.)

For he's a jolly good fellow
For he's a jolly good fellow
For he's a jolly good fe-el-low
Which nobody can deny!

I wouldn't have that dog as a gift anyway! Judy! Oh, Judy! My pretty Judy! Jugi dear, Ju-ju! Darling! Ducky!

Judy (enters with stick tied in her hand): Well, what do you want, now that I've come?

Punch (turns to audience): Ah! What a pretty little creature! Isn't she one beauty? She has blue eyes and pearly nose—no, pearly hair, and curly teeth—I mean hair. Oh, you know what I mean.

Punch (turning to Judy): Why, Judy, I want to dance with you, my Ducky! (He grabs Judy, and singing a tune, they dance together. At conclusion of dance, Punch hits Judy with stick.)

Judy: You villain! How dare you strike me! (Strikes Punch with her stick.) Take that, and that, and that!

Punch (turns to audience): Ah! What did I tell you, she's always so playful! (Turns to Judy.) Bring me the baby, my Ducky!

Judy (exits, then returns with the baby): Now, be sure you take good care of the baby. Don't make him cry.

Punch: Who me? Now get out, woman! Get out! (Pushes Judy off stage. Pats baby on head, then rocks him in his arms and sings.)

Rock-a-bye baby in the tree top

When the wind blows the cradle will rock

When the bough breaks the cradle will fall

And down will come baby, cradle, and all.

What a pretty baby he is. Little Ducky! (Shows baby to audience.) Never was there such a baby! He looks just like his father. Beautiful nose—what a nose! And look at his chin, his chimny, chin, chin. Ah-goo! Ah-goo! Pretty little baby!

Baby (cries): Waaaa, Mamaaaa!

Judy, looking very much like Punch with her curved nose and chin, wears a gingham apron.

Punch (thumps baby with stick): Go to sleep, my pretty!

Baby (cries louder): Wa-a-a-a-a! Mama-a-a-a!

Punch (whacks baby harder with stick): Go to sleep, I tell you! There, my pretty. Doesn't he take after his father?

Baby (catches hold of Punch's nose): Wa-a-a-a-a! Mama-a-a-a!

Punch: Let go my nose! Murderer! Oh, my pretty nose! My poor nose! There, you bad baby, go to your mother! (Throws baby off the stage. Sings and dances around stage.)

For he's a jolly good fellow

For he's a jolly good fellow

For he's a jolly good fe-el-low

Which nobody can deny.

Judy (enters with stick): Where's the baby?

Punch: Why, didn't you catch him?

Judy: Catch him! What have you done with him?

Punch: Oh! I just threw him out of the window. I thought you might be passing by and caught him.

Judy (shrieks): Oh, you horrid wretch! You shall pay for this! (Strikes Punch with stick.) I'll teach you to drop my child out of the window. Take this, and this, and this! Police! Police! Police!

Punch (holds head with hands while Judy strikes him): Ow-w-w-w! Stop it! Stop it! I'll never do it again!

Judy (still striking): I'll teach you! I'll teach you!

Punch (strikes Judy with stick): Then I'll be teacher too! (Whacks Judy so hard over the head that she sinks to the floor dead.) There, that will teach you! (Kicks Judy off the stage.) Good riddance to you too. (Sings and dances around stage.)

For he's a jolly good fellow

The Baby resembles his parents, with a curved nose and turned-up chin. He wears a lace cap.

For he's a jolly good fellow
For he's a jolly good fe-el-low
Which nobody can deny.

Policeman (enters with a club): Hello! Hello! Hello! Here I am!

Punch: Hello! Hello! Hello! Here I am, too! (Whacks policeman with stick.)

Policeman (points club at Punch): Do you see my club, Sir?

Punch: Do you feel my stick, Sir? (Whacks policeman again.)

Policeman (shoves Punch away): Take your nose out of my face, Sir!

Punch: Take your face out of my nose, Sir!

Policeman: Mr. Punch, I've come for you!

Punch: What for?

Policeman: I've come to take you to jail!

Punch: To jail!

Policeman: Yes, for murdering your baby.

Punch: To jail for a little thing like that?

Policeman: Yes, and for murdering your wife too!

Punch: Well, she was *my* wife, wasn't she?

Policeman: Yes, and for Scaramouch too!

Punch: Well, he got in my way!

Policeman: You've committed a crime, Sir! And I've come to take you up! (Moves towards Punch.)

Punch: And I've come to knock you down! (Whacks policeman down, then sings and dances.) For he's a jolly good fellow, For he's a jolly good fellow, For he's a jolly good fe-el-low, Which nobody can deny.

Policeman (rises): Mr. Punch, I don't like that noise!

Punch (mimics policeman): Mr. Punch, I don't like that noise! What noise?

The Policeman, fat with a double chin, turned-up nose, big mouth, and a brushlike moustache, sports a badge and brass buttons on his blue costume.

Policeman: That horrid bad noise you're making. I'll have no more of it!
Punch: You won't, will you? (Repeats louder.) For he's

179 ☞

a jolly good fellow; For he's a jolly good fellow; For he's a jolly good fe-el-low; Which nobody can deny! Not like my sweet music! (Punch cracks the policeman over the head.) Take that! And that! And that! (Policeman falls dead. Punch touches him with his foot. Policeman doesn't move.) Well, that's the end of him. Out you go with the others! (Punch pushes him off stage. Then sings and dances around.)

For he's a jolly good fellow
For he's a jolly good fellow
For he's a jolly good fe-el-low
Which nobody can deny.

Hangman (enters carrying the gallows): Mr. Punch!

Punch: Who are *you*?

Hangman: I'm the hangman and you are my prisoner. You have broken the laws of our country and I have come to hang you!

Punch: Broken the laws? I couldn't break them. I never even touched them!

Hangman: I have come to hang you up!

Punch: Hang *me*?

Hangman: I said *you*. Now get ready.

Punch: How do I get ready?

Hangman: By saying your prayers.

Punch: Which prayers?

Hangman: I don't care which prayers. Any prayers.

Punch (frightened): Oh, dear! Oh, dear! Spare me! I have a wife and sixteen small children. (Whines.) What will they do without me?

Hangman: Come here!

Punch (bends down to stroke his leg): I can't. I've a broken bone in my leg and can't walk.

The Hangman wears a black mask over his eyes so no one will recognize him, and a long, pointed black cap.

Hangman: Then, I must fetch you! (The two struggle, hangman takes Punch over to gallows.) Put your head in here! (Points to looped rope.)

Punch: I don't know how. I was never hanged before.

Hangman: Why, it's easy. Just put your head through this noose.

Punch: Which noose?

Hangman: This noose, booby!

Punch: Which head?

Hangman: Your head, of course!

Punch: Well, how?

Hangman: Here, see? I'll show you how! (Hangman puts his own head into noose.)

Punch (quickly pulls the rope and hangs the hangman): Oee! Oee! Now that's the end of you Mr. Hangman! (Kicks hangman off the stage, then sings and dances with glee.)

    For he's a jolly good fellow

    For he's a jolly good fellow

    For he's a jolly good fe-el-low

    Which nobody can deny.

Devil (enters without Punch noticing him.)

Punch (senses the devil's presence, but every time he turns around the devil turns behind him): Fe-fi-fo-fum! I smell fire! (Turns fast, but no luck. Turns slowly, but no luck again.)

Devil (pops down, pops up again in front of Punch): Here I am. I have come for you! (Pins Punch to wall.)

Punch (frightened): Ooh! Ooh! Not good little me! Not little me!

Devil: Yes! I have come for you, Mr. Punch!

Punch: Oooooh! Mr. *Punch*! *That* wicked fellow! Oh, yes, there he is. Down there! What a villain! Had to hang him just today! Oh, yes, take him along by all means!

Devil (looks down to where hangman is): Thank you, Sir! Thank you! (Makes his exit.)

Punch: You are welcome, Sir! (Dances and sings.)

    Fiddle-dee-dee! Fiddle-dee-dee!

    Cat's in the corner, can't catch me!

Now all my foes are put to flight. (Turns to audience.)
Ladies and Gentlemen all, good-by to the adventures
of Mr. Punch! (Exits with stick over his shoulder
singing.)
For he's a jolly good fellow
For he's a jolly good fellow
For he's a jolly good fe-el-low
Which nobody can deny.

The Devil, ugly and bony, with horns, pointed ears, and a beard,
wears a fiery-red costume.

A Visit from Outer Space

(An Original Play)

Note: Using this play, see what you can do with creating your own puppets to fit the story.

Characters:

Cosmo, a spaceman
Celeste, a spacewoman
Earth man
1st Astronaut
2nd Astronaut

Properties:

Spaceship—exterior view, flat model attached to long rod
Spaceship—interior view, three-dimensional model
Automobile—can either be a three-dimensional model or
    a flat model attached to a short rod
Navigation chart

At Curtain Rise:

Spaceship is speeding across sky in a zigzag motion. It is obvious that something is wrong and it is about to make a crash landing. Then: Bong! Bang! Thrump! Creeek! Crash! A moment of silence.

Cosmo (appearing from behind the wrecked spaceship):
    Are you all right, Celeste?

Celeste (also appearing from behind the spaceship): Yes,
    Cosmo, I'm all right. But for goodness sake, what
    happened?

Cosmo: The rocket motor conked out.

Celeste (looking around): Where are we?

Cosmo (also looking around): I think this is the sky object called Earth.

Celeste (incredulous): You mean that place where all those strange creatures live?

Cosmo (reluctantly): I'm afraid so.

Celeste (frightened): Cosmo, I'm frightened. Get me home quickly! (Earth man appears who walks across stage.) Eeeeks! Here's one coming now! Please try to fix the motor.

Cosmo (goes over to spaceship and pokes around for a while): Bad news, Celeste. I can't do a thing with the rocket motor.

Celeste (frantic): You mean we have to stay here forever? Oh, Cosmo, we can't do that. We'll die if we stay here! Think of something.

Cosmo: Don't rush me. I'm thinking. I'm thinking. (He pokes around spaceship again and pulls out a chart from behind it.) Here, I've got the chart. Now, let's see where we are exactly. (He looks at chart, then suddenly he raises his head.) Ahhh! The chart shows us that we're not far from an earth space port. Let's find it and see what we can do. Hurry! Let's go! (The two space travelers set out hand in hand to find the space port. Curtain closes.)

Act II

At Curtain Rise:

A space port on earth. In a corner is an interior model of a spaceship with two astronauts seated at the controls. The two space travelers appear, hand in hand. As they look around, an automobile suddenly speeds by and disappears.

Celeste: Yikes! Cosmo, what was that???

Cosmo: I don't know. But those two lights were sure blinding. It almost knocked us down. And the noise and smell were awful! I guess it was one of those auto things. Our people stopped using those centuries ago. Hurry, hurry, we'll be at the space port soon. (They see the space rocket which is about to take off.)

1st Astronaut: Count down! Ten, nine, eight, seven . . .

Cosmo: Now stay close to me. We have to get aboard that spaceship without being seen.

Celeste: Oh, Cosmo, I'm scared.

Cosmo: Shhhhhhh!

1st Astronaut: Six, five (Cosmo and Celeste manage to jump aboard), four, three, two, one, lift off! (Spaceship remains on ground since the rest takes place in the interior.)

Cosmo (whispering): Here we go. Now we're zooming into space. When I give the signal, we'll present ourselves. O.K. Now! (Louder) Hello!

1st Astronaut (turns around and sees Cosmo and Celeste for the first time. Very much surprised): You! Who are you? How did you get here?

Cosmo: Our spaceship broke down on Earth and we thought you wouldn't mind giving us a lift back into space. You see, we come from space. Our home is far beyond the moon.

2nd Astronaut: Gosh! Aren't you queer-looking ones though!

Cosmo (indignantly): Ha! Look who's talking. We haven't seen anyone as queer-looking as you Earth people. And you two fellows, especially! Ugh!

1st Astronaut: Well, now that you are here, what are

we going to do with you? We certainly can't land you anywhere. At least, not yet. And we certainly don't want to take you on our entire journey back to Earth. Can't stand the sight of you that long! Ha, ha, ha!

Cosmo: Don't worry, the feeling is mutual. We can't stand looking at you either. In fact, I think I'm about to become sick—Oooops! Just drop us off in space. We'll manage to get home then, on our own.

Celeste: Oh, Cosmo! Are you sure?

2nd Astronaut: How will you get home on your own?

Cosmo: We'll just float along in space until one of our rocket ships comes along to pick us up.

1st Astronaut: O.K. In five minutes we'll be five hundred miles from here. How will that do?

Cosmo: Fine!

2nd Astronaut: My, but you're funny-looking!

Celeste: You're funny too!

1st Astronaut: All right! Here we are. Are you sure you'll be O.K?

Cosmo: Don't worry about us, we'll be fine.

1st Astronaut: All right. Out you both go. You're on your own. Good-by!

Cosmo and Celeste (jump out one at a time): Good-by! Thanks for the lift! (The two space travelers disappear.)

2nd Astronaut: What a way to travel! (Curtain draws.)

Epilogue

Puppets and the Future

The future in puppetry holds tremendous possibilities. Today, we are turning our creative minds to experimenting with materials and techniques never before dreamed of in puppetry.

Now, anything that can be made to move becomes a potential puppet. Many natural materials such as bamboo, clay, metals, fruits, sponges, leaves, bird feathers, and even vegetables can be used for puppet making.

Also many objects and materials invented by man, such as umbrellas, spools, wires, and figures from folded newspaper are being used.

Some professional puppeteers are experimenting with intricate lights and colors, for example, drawing paper painted with transparent dyes which will show up in color on the shadow screen. Also clear and colored acetate is cut and tissue paper with cellulose varnish is stuck to it. Colored tissue paper in two layers of adhesive plastic is another type of material being experimented with.

All puppets are easy to make by using materials found in the classroom or at home. With this in mind see what you can do to give puppetry the fascinating, creative expression that rightfully belongs to this art.

Some Other Useful Books

Adair, Margaret Weeks. *Do-it-in-a-Day Puppets for Beginners.* New York: John Day Company, 1964

Cummings, Richard. *101 Hand Puppets.* New York: David McKay Company, 1962.

Howard, Vernon. *Puppet and Pantomime Plays.* New York: Sterling Publishing Company, 1962.

Jagendorf, Moritz. *Puppets for Beginners.* Boston: Plays, Inc. Publishers, 1952.

Lewis, Shari. *The Shari Lewis Puppet Book.* New York: The Citadel Press, 1958.

Pels, Gertrude. *Easy Puppets.* New York: Thomas Y. Crowell Company, 1951.

Tichenor, Tom. *Folk Plays for Puppets You Can Make.* New York: Abingdon Press, 1959.

Index